TRULY, MADLY, DEEPLY LOVE YOU

HOW TO LOVE YOURSELF BY IMPROVING SELF-ESTEEM AND SELF-CONFIDENCE

ATHENA HARMONIA

ATHENA HARMONIA

Truly, Madly, Deeply Love YOU

How to love yourself by improving self esteem and self confidence

First edition

This book was professionally typeset on Reedsy.
Find out more at reedsy.com

Contents

Introduction   1

   The Most Important Relationship in Your Life   1

Chapter 1: What Is Self-Love Anyway?   5

   The 10 Selves in Self-Love   7

   The Power of Self-Love   11

Chapter 2: How to Kick Self-Loathing's Butt   15

   What Is Self-Loathing?   15

   Exercises to Stop Self-Loathing   20

Chapter 3: Building Positive Connections   25

   Building Self-Love While in a Relationship   25

   Self-Love and How it Affects Friendships   28

   How to Walk Away From Toxic Relationships   30

   Building Positive Relationships   33

Chapter 4: Telling Depression to F*** Off   36

   The Relationship Between Self-Love and Depression   38

   Accepting Positivity From Others   40

   Exercises to Treat Symptoms of Depression   43

Chapter 5: Loving Your Self-Image and Your Body   46

   What Are Self-Image and Body Image?   47

   Where Do Insecurities Come From?   50

   Exercises to Improve Self-Love and Body Acceptance   53

Chapter 6: Social Media and Its Delicious Poison   56

   Social Media and Self-Love   56

   Caring Too Much About What Others Think   60

   Exercises to Treat Social Media's Poison   62

Chapter 7: Loving Your Failings and Achievements   66

Self-Worth and Self-Love   66
Why Failing Is Important   68
How to Learn From Failure   69
How to Acknowledge and Appreciate Achievements   71
Exercises to Increase Self-Worth   72
Chapter 8: Affirmations   75
How to Create and Use Affirmations   77
Benefits of Affirmations   80
Affirmations for Self-Love   81
Please Leave A Review   84
Conclusion   86
Loving Yourself   86
References   88

Introduction

The Most Important Relationship in Your Life

Did you know about 85% of the worldwide population is influenced by their self-esteem and struggles with how they view themselves (Guttman, 2019)? This statistic is shockingly high and shows that you are not alone in your struggle for self-love and self-respect. You may wonder why this number or fact should matter to you. Sometimes it is comforting and affirming to know others understand and can relate to what you are going through. I remember dealing with many self-love issues, which caused me a lot of distress. I suffered for a long time before speaking to a friend about it. Having someone to confide in was helpful and comforting by itself. As it turned out, my friend was struggling with self-love in many of the same ways, and she opened up to me in return. Knowing someone else was struggling like me made me realize I was not alone and empowered me to overcome our shared pain. If you are struggling with self-love issues, remember you are not alone. Self-love is a global issue, with many people struggling against it and triumphing over it daily.

Another statistic you may find shocking is approximately eight out of ten women have expressed trouble with their self-esteem (Social, n.d.). It is scary to deal with self-love issues, but much less so when you know you are not in this battle alone. If you are a woman, please understand that your fellow women can sympathize with your struggles and offer their support and kindness. And even if you are not a woman, knowing how many people struggle alongside you can be motivating and inspiring. This knowledge will push you to keep working toward improved self-love and self-esteem. Come one, come all! This book is about you! This book explains why loving yourself can be challenging but worthwhile and how you can effectively improve your self-confidence and self-esteem. Loving you and who you are is essential to life and the key to happiness.

If you neglect your self-love, your entire quality of life may suffer. However, despite this, self-love often gets overlooked and dismissed. If you were to take stock of your life right now and list your priorities, self-love would probably be at the bottom, if it even made the priority list. Unfortunately, it is common for self-love to be at the bottom of priorities. Today's society emphasizes and values more on academic achievements, progressing your career, filial piety, and romantic relationships. You are probably so focused on your relationships with others that you have neglected the most crucial relationship in your life. Your relationship with YOU! Remembering to stay on top of social gatherings with friends or family, work emails and meetings, anniversaries, and birthdays is a lot to juggle. It is normal to realize you have not consciously worked on self-love. However, this can create a few problems in your life.

When you lack self-love, many other things will be affected, such as your self-esteem, self-appreciation, and self-confidence. These little cracks can cause various other areas of your life to crumble. For example, you will be less confident and less assertive in your love life, making you more vulnerable to being used, exploited, or manipulated. A lack of self-love will strain even the most perfect relationships because poor communication skills hinder productive discussions. You may develop self-defeating attitudes or people-pleasing habits preventing honest and open communication. In your professional life, your lack of self-love may get in the way of your upward mobility. You will need more confidence to be a leader or voice your opinions and ideas, putting you at a disadvantage against others who are more confident.

A lack of self-love can harm various aspects of your life and decrease the quality of your relationships, leading to feelings of depression, anxiety, or even self-loathing. You may be plagued by thoughts such as, I hate myself; why cannot I be better? Why did I say that? I'm stupid, or even Everyone would be happier if I wasn't here. Having thoughts like these daily can be extremely uncomfortable and distressing. It is essential to address and improve your self-love quickly.

Quickly addressing and improving your self-love is precisely what you will achieve through this book. You will learn what it takes to love yourself and improve your relationships. While also learning techniques you can use throughout your life to enhance the love you feel toward yourself. Of course, this learning process will be challenging. But with the tips, strategies, and knowledge provided here, you are guaranteed to gain access to the simplest and most effective ways to build up your self-love. All the tools are here in this book — all you need to bring to the table is the commitment and dedication to keep using them.

Before you start, let's get an overview of the various tools you will gain. Briefly put, you will learn where self-love comes from, how to eliminate your self-loathing, how to improve your relationships, and how to deal with your symptoms of depression. In addition, you will also explore your self-image and how to love your body, the impact of social media, how to accept your strengths and weaknesses, and affirmations to support your self-love journey. All this information will be vital to your success and help you cultivate more self-love, self-esteem, and self-confidence.

In my late twenties, I was in a deep depression without a hint of self-love, and my life felt like it was at its end. I could not connect with anyone around me, and I could not understand why all my relationships were deteriorating. These failing relationships only added to my self-love issues, and I began to blame and hate myself. During this steep descent into darkness, I started researching and practicing the methods I will share in this book. I am confident the information here can help you achieve all this because I have personally used these techniques and knowledge. With it all, I overcame my self-love issues and created a new life.

The struggle for self-love, confidence, and esteem is an uphill climb. Being past the worst of it, I can look back and feel grateful for my experiences. Once

I learned how to love myself, I wanted to teach others the same. Helping you achieve true love for yourself matters deeply to me. I am about to give you the same tools I used to get out of my depression, build up my self-love, and even repair my relationships. I have written this book for you because I know it can help. If you have been dealing with depression and self-love issues, I have been there, and I understand how it feels.

Chapter 1: What Is Self-Love Anyway?

The first step to obtaining self-love is to understand what exactly it entails. You need to know what you are aiming for to hit the target. Imagine someone sent you to the mall to buy something they needed, but they did not tell you what it was. You would walk around blindly, pick up something unrelated, or even pass by what they needed. It is best if you come to understand self-love thoroughly to be more purposeful, confident, and directed in your efforts to achieve it.

Self-love is the appreciation, respect, and devotion you feel for yourself. These feelings can typically be created, supported, and maintained through specific actions to advocate for personal, physical, mental, and spiritual growth. When you love yourself, you will want to work toward and protect your emotional well-being and happiness. It does not mean you only care about yourself and disregard others. It means you will respect and advocate for your needs and wants, considering your values, boundaries, and limits. You will care for your needs without sacrificing your values, ideals, boundaries, or self-respect to please others. You will know what you deserve and fight to defend yourself. For example, suppose someone is mistreating you, with self-love you will be able to tell yourself you deserve to be treated with respect enabling you to protect yourself and not accept disrespectful treatment.

Self-love can be interpreted in many ways, and self-love can look different from case to case. Self-love, in the broadest sense, means you take care of yourself and advocate for yourself because you believe you have worth. Everyone has different needs, values, and wants, so they will have different ways of looking out for themselves.

Now, you must figure out what self-love would look like for you. If you accept yourself as a person of worth, what basic needs do you want to have met? What desires do you want to pursue? What things become unacceptable for you? How do you want others to treat you? How do you want to treat yourself? What about yourself do you want to change or improve? All these questions can help you start exploring what self-love means to you.

If you are still unsure, here are some examples to inspire you on what self-love can look like. For starters, self-love can be talking to and about yourself with respect, kindness, and consideration. You do not put yourself down in front of others or upset yourself with your thoughts. Self-love can also be about prioritizing yourself, meaning you start putting yourself first rather than always giving in to others. Which in turn also trains your assertiveness, helping you become true to yourself.

Sometimes, you may sacrifice who you are and what you believe in to please others. Self-love tells you it is okay to say no to others when you are uncomfortable or disagree with them. As well as this, self-love can mean stopping your judgmental and self-critical thoughts. Instead, treat yourself with kindness and understanding, even when you mess up. Self-love can also mean setting healthy boundaries to ensure others do not offend or make you uncomfortable. Boundaries are a great way to respect yourself and your emotions. Another form of self-love is to forgive yourself. You may often be too hard on yourself and overemphasize your flaws. Self-love says to forgive yourself, learn from your mistakes, and move on.

One significant way you can love yourself more is to practice self-care. Self-care is exactly what it sounds like: it means to take care of your physical and mental well-being. Self-care can come from stretching, exercising, taking breaks from work, eating a healthy snack, connecting with others, engaging in your hobby, or doing something creative. All this can improve your self-love as it informs you that your physical, emotional, and mental well-being are essential and you are worthy of love and care.

The 10 Selves in Self-Love

To further understand self-love, let's break it down into 10 components. Self-love encompasses:

1. Self-awareness
2. Self-acceptance
3. Self-care
4. Self-compassion
5. Self-trust
6. Self-esteem
7. Self-empowerment
8. Self-respect
9. Self-pleasure
10. Self-expression

Of course, you do not have to work through each component to obtain self-love. The good thing is all these components are interlinked. When you improve on one, another will likely improve as well. For example, when you increase your self-respect, your self-care will also improve.

Do not feel overwhelmed by these 10 components, thinking you have gone from 1 focus to 10. Instead, think of this as a way for you to understand self-love even more. Gaining this in-depth knowledge will help you be more aware of your areas for growth as you pursue self-love. While you continue down this path, you can keep these components at the forefront of your mind and assess your progress. You may have made leaps and bounds in self-empowerment, but you must still work on self-expression. In this way, the 10 selves of self-love are not extra work for you but simply an extension and supplement to your understanding of self-love. Without further delay, let's start to understand each of these 10 elements:

1. **Self-awareness**: This has to do with how honest you are with yourself and how aware you are of your thoughts, emotions, values, beliefs,

boundaries, and standards. When you are aware of all these things, it will be easier to be true to yourself. You cannot be true to yourself if you do not know who you are. Self-awareness can also help you track how the things around you affect you and alert you to notice when you are uncomfortable. Also, one thing to note here is standards are different from expectations. Expectations are limits you impose on yourself based on external values of worth. At the same time, standards are loving thoughts to protect your sense of worth.

2. **Self-acceptance**: This entails loving yourself unconditionally and accepting every part of yourself, the good and the bad, your strengths and weaknesses. To practice self-acceptance, try to think of a part of yourself you do not particularly like and accept it as part of who you are. You can always change this part of you, but it is still important to accept it. Self-acceptance and self-awareness go hand and hand. You cannot use self-acceptance to accept yourself without knowing who you are. This is because you need self-awareness to know yourself.

3. **Self-care**: As we covered previously, is the act of taking care of your mental, emotional, and physical well-being to ensure you feel healthy, happy, and whole.

4. **Self-compassion**: This component helps you forgive yourself when you make mistakes. Rather than immediately condemning and judging yourself. Self-compassion will lead you to treat yourself like a friend. This way, you will address yourself with kindness and understanding. You will understand, accept, and be sympathetic to who you are, where you are in life, and how you feel.

5. **Self-trust**: Have you ever been paralyzed by thoughts telling you, you can't do it, you're going to fail, or you're in an impossible situation? Well, these thoughts are part of your self-doubt, and the opposite of self-doubt is self-trust. When you trust yourself, you will have confidence in your abilities and capacity to overcome obstacles and survive the difficult things in life. Self-trust is a vital part of your relationship with yourself. It can make you feel more comfortable and confident in your skin and help you distinguish between your fears and your authentic self. Self-

doubt will lead you to believe in the thoughts led by fear, but self-trust will lead you to believe in the ideas led by your true self, which is made up of pure and loving energy.

6. **Self-esteem**: How much do you believe in your abilities and worth? When you believe in yourself more, you will be more confident in being yourself in front of others. But when you do not believe in yourself and have low self-esteem, you are more likely to bend backward trying to please others or try to fit in with others even though you disagree with them.

7. **Self-empowerment**: Learning how you can motivate yourself to chase down what you want. No matter who you want to be, what you want to do, where you want to go, or how you want to go about things, self-empowerment is the driving force encouraging you to go for it and to live out your dreams. Self-empowerment will tell you, you deserve to get what you desire, and as long as you put in the effort, you can achieve what you want.

8. **Self-respect**: This has to do with how you treat yourself. Do you do things to make yourself feel safe, honored, and validated, or do you do things that make you feel threatened, vulnerable, unseen, and unheard? What kind of treatment do you accept? What are your standards for yourself? If you let others pass off their workload to you, even if you do not want to do the extra work, you are not respecting yourself because you are allowing yourself to be taken advantage of. Suppose you stay in an unhappy relationship because you are scared to be alone. In that case, you are not respecting yourself because you are not looking out for your long-term happiness. Self-respect can be a tricky path to follow, but the main goal is to do things to make you feel happy, healthy, and safe. Self-respect often interacts with self-esteem because when you do not respect yourself, you are not being true to yourself. Eventually, this can make you lose confidence in your abilities and worth.

9. **Self-pleasure**: Often, the most accessible component of self-love is self-pleasure. As it only asks you to do things you enjoy. Simple enough? Do something to make yourself happy. You will have to make time for

your hobbies and interests. Though, of course, do them in moderation and not indulge in anything harmful to you in the long run.

10. **Self-expression**: This component has to do with being true to yourself. You deserve to express your opinions and beliefs in whatever ways you want (as long as they are respectful). But remember, self-expression has more to do with giving yourself a voice and less to do with convincing others of your opinions. You are not trying to convince or convert anyone; you are simply putting your truth out there. During this process, you may find some like-minded people who can become a community for you. Self-expression is essential because when you have no room to express yourself, you cannot be true to yourself, and your self-esteem may take a hit.

As you strive to improve your self-love, you can zoom in and understand the various components of self-love you are enhancing and single out the components that still need more work. Hopefully, now, with the understanding of the 10 selves in self-love, you can understand why each is important. Keeping these selves in mind, you can track your progress in each one. In doing this, you can make your efforts more precise and effective.

Before you move on to the next section, here are some quick tips on making your self-love journey much more effective and efficient. The first tip is to identify your "why." Why are you starting on this journey? Why is self-love vital to you right now? Why would improving self-love benefit you? Discovering your "why" will help you remain emotionally committed to your efforts in self-love and help keep you motivated when times are hard. Another tip is to try to forgive. The opposite of love is hate; how can you cultivate self-love if you are still harboring resentment and anger in your heart?

It is in your best interest to forgive whoever you are angry at, be it yourself or others. Doing so will significantly benefit your self-love journey. Keep in mind forgiveness does not mean you are condoning certain behaviors. All you are doing is freeing yourself from the mental burden of hate and empowering yourself to move on. One last tip is to recognize you have all the power in this journey to self-love. No one else can control how you see and treat yourself, and no one else can control your thoughts and actions. It is all up to you. It is your life. Do not see yourself as a victim but as the owner of all your thoughts, emotions, and actions. You are in control, and you are deciding to love yourself more.

The Power of Self-Love

Now that you understand self-love more, let's prepare for all the benefits you will receive once you cultivate more self-love. Whenever you are feeling down in the dumps and ready to give up on self-love, think about all the benefits you are about to explore. The benefits are one way to keep your eye on the prize! Understanding the power of self-love can help prepare you for the positive changes to come and help keep you motivated.

One great power of self-love is it can help reduce your stress. This power utilizes the self-care component of self-love a lot. When you have self-love, you will take better care of yourself to ensure you are not overworking and heading toward a burnout. If you notice you are feeling stressed, your self-care will kick in, and you will take the necessary actions to reduce your stress. Examples include taking breaks from work, hanging out with friends, or splitting the workload more fairly. Whatever your chosen method, your self-love will enable you to take better care of yourself so your stress doesn't get out of hand. Without self-love, you may not realize you are stressed, and you may push yourself toward a mental breakdown.

Next, self-love can help you develop healthier habits, and this has to do with the self-awareness component of self-love. When you are more aware of your behaviors and tendencies, you can be more honest and open with yourself, recognizing when a particular habit is doing more harm than good. This awareness can help you make healthier decisions and positive life changes. Of course, bad habits are hard to break. Still, the self-empowerment component of your self-love can motivate and propel you to make and sustain these healthy changes in your life. Your self-compassion can support you as you make these changes by preventing you from judging yourself for having those bad habits in the first place and encouraging you to develop new, better practices to be kinder to yourself.

Other than being healthier, self-love can improve your emotional resilience. Emotional resilience is your ability to bounce back, withstand, and survive difficult times and distressing emotions. Without emotional resilience, you may easily despair whenever something goes wrong. Despair can make every obstacle you face into an insurmountable mountain, crushing your spirit, while also draining your energy and confidence. It is an uncomfortable and ineffective way to live. Thankfully, self-love helps you avoid this. When you have self-love, you will not blame yourself for your hardships. Instead, you will be able to see the big picture and gain a better perspective of things. Whenever you face difficulties, you will remember it is not the end of the world, and you have the resources and ability to overcome whatever is in your way. Increasing your ability to handle hardships further prepares you for the challenges you may face in the future.

As promised, self-love can even improve your relationships. Previously, you briefly explored how a lack of self-love can harm your relationships. How can you love another if you do not know how to love yourself? When you love yourself, it becomes much easier to love others. You can love others from a purer, more sincere place. When you do not have self-love, you may love others to get their validation and to verify your worth.

Unfortunately, this creates an unhealthy and reliant relationship where you may be insecure, needy, and have no boundaries. But once you establish yourself in self-love, you can love others without being reliant on them, making you more stable, confident, and considerate. You will be able to stand up for yourself in relationships and even end them if you know they are unhealthy. Overall, self-love can improve how you interact with others and help you realize what relationships you want to keep or not.

Self-love even makes you more productive, returning to your self-empowerment, self-compassion, and self-trust. A lot of the time, people tend to procrastinate when they are feeling doubt. Procrastinators are still determining if they can succeed with the task at hand and then put it off and do nothing. Or they are unsure of their decision, and they become frozen in doubt and overthinking. Procrastination obviously kills your productivity. Self-love counteracts this by using kind words to motivate you and using your confidence and trust in your abilities to propel you forward into action. Self-compassion can even increase your emotional resilience by comforting you, letting you know that you can still learn from your mistakes and improve even if you mess up or fail. Once you are free from your criticism and judgments, you will be freer to make changes.

Anxiety and depression symptoms can be managed through self-love as well—a big win for your mental health. The component of self-love playing the most prominent role in combating signs of anxiety and depression is self-compassion. Many thoughts brought on by depression and anxiety are self-deprecating and self-defeating. Self-compassion can reverse these effects by treating you with kindness and understanding. I am not saying people who feel anxious or depressed are incapable of self-love. You can feel those symptoms while still fighting to improve your self-love. And once you do, you can use self-love as a weapon to fight against your symptoms of anxiety and depression, both empowering and affirming yourself.

Self-love can also increase your happiness by decreasing your thoughts of self-blame, self-doubt, self-criticism, and self-deprecation, all of which lower your quality of life and steal your joy. When caught up in self-blame, self-criticism, and the like, you will always be focused on your flaws, limits, mistakes, and weaknesses. However, when you have self-love, you will focus more on your strengths, healthy boundaries, growth opportunities, and desires. You will be more ready to stand up for yourself and chase what you want, preventing you from being mistreated and increasing your chances of getting what you want. All this can lead to higher satisfaction in life.

Self-love can encourage you to stop criticizing yourself and recognize your worth and abilities. On another note, self-love can boost your confidence. When you are stuck in a loop of self-criticism, you will be solely focused on your flaws and get very depressed every time you make a mistake. Feeling this way can harm your self-esteem and self-trust, making it hard to act confidently.

In tandem with that, self-love can empower you to achieve your goals. You will be more confident and motivated to chase down what you want and will no longer be shackled by self-doubt, stress, and self-defeating thoughts. You will be freer to know what you want and to fight for it.

Finally, self-love has the power to inspire others. One significant hindrance to self-love is the misconception of self-love being selfish. This misleading belief may keep you from genuinely aspiring for self-love because you do not want to be selfish. Discard this misconception right now! Self-love is not selfish. It can help others by inspiring them to love themselves too. When they observe you and see all the benefits above, they may become motivated to chase down self-love for themselves, highlighting why self-love can benefit those around you, not only yourself.

Self-love is a healthy trait to develop. It should not be confused with egoism or narcissism because it is neither arrogant nor self-indulgent. Love, when expressed in the right way, should never be unhealthy. And self-love, in the forms you have and will be learning, is a pure, sincere expression of your care for yourself. Of course, this should be held in tandem with consideration and respect for those around you. An unhealthy and misguided expression of self-love would be to use self-love as an excuse to run away from responsibilities or to treat others poorly. To be clear, this is not self-love. Self-love is only your actions to treat yourself with care, respect, and honesty. These things do not mean you are selfish. They tell you to recognize your worth, which is a great thing to do.

In the next chapter, you will explore another possible obstacle to self-love: self-loathing. You will also discover how to leave it behind while moving onward and upward.

Chapter 2: How to Kick Self-Loathing's Butt

Everyone has had self-loathing thoughts before. They come in the forms of *I look ugly today, I'm stupid,* or *I wish I were anybody else.* These thoughts can harm your mental health as they deny, reject, and criticize who you are, convincing you that you are worthless and even potentially making you sad or angry. You may be sad because you feel worthless or angry because of intense hatred toward yourself. Whatever the outcome, self-loathing can be a distressing experience. In this chapter, you will learn how to kick self-loathing's butt and leave it in your dust!

What Is Self-Loathing?

As with self-love, you must understand self-loathing more thoroughly to combat it properly. Self-loathing is your negative feelings, thoughts, and attitudes toward yourself. It may manifest itself in the forms of self-doubt, self-hatred, or feelings of worthlessness. You may have trouble believing in your abilities, get upset when you make minor mistakes, or feel like you have no value and no reason to treat yourself well. You may also have a very negative self-image and a shallow perception of yourself. Every thought you have of yourself will be putting yourself down, judging yourself, or ridiculing yourself. Harsh self-criticism will target your beliefs, achievements, strengths, personality, and other traits you may be unable to change about yourself. It may also mean you blame yourself more often than not when things go wrong, even when your actions have nothing to do with how things ended up. You will look for any reason to start criticizing yourself again, whether or not it is backed by logic or reason. And even when things go right, you may look for reasons to be upset at yourself, and you will not accept any positive feedback or praise from others.

These are the various ways self-loathing can present itself in your life, and there are many other ways each person may express their self-loathing. Remember to look for recurring negative feelings, thoughts, and attitudes toward yourself. If you are still unsure if you are experiencing self-loathing, try to check your tendencies against the following symptoms. These are a few negative thought patterns often affecting those with self-loathing. These thoughts can amplify the hate you feel for yourself and keep you stuck in a loop of negativity and despair:

- **All-or-nothing thinking**: When you experience all-or-nothing thinking, you perceive things as black and white, good or bad, perfect or flawed. Catastrophizing certain circumstances increase your stress and exaggerates the cost of your mistakes. For example, if you missed a few questions on an exam, you will not be able to see the middle ground where you scored well but have room for improvement. Instead, you will only see the extremes, where because it was not a perfect score, it was a total failure, and thus you are a failure, and you will probably fail the entire course. Do you see how your thoughts can spiral with all-or-nothing thinking? There is no room for gray areas, and your life will be lived according to stringent, very nonsensical rules.
- **Filtering**: This is another negative thought pattern increasing your negativity and pessimism. Thinking in terms of filtering is like wearing a pair of glasses to filter out all the good things happening to you and only leaving in and focusing on all the bad things happening. Thinking this way negates and dismisses all the positive aspects of your day. Instead, you are choosing to emphasize all the negative parts. For example, imagine one day you finished all your work early, got praised by your boss, and even spent some time with your friends after work. However, once you

got home, you stubbed your toe. Filtering would cause you to forget or disregard all the happy things you experienced during the day. Instead, all you would remember would be stubbing your toe. This form of thinking can put you in a bad, pessimistic mood, no matter how many good things the world puts in your path.

- **Emotional reasoning**: This negative thought pattern involves believing your emotions are accurate reflections of reality. It is a form of thinking that disregards all logic and reason, leading you to believe in things without properly interrogating the truth. Suddenly, you believe negative things about yourself, leading to misunderstandings in relationships. For example, if you talk with your friend and feel they are mad at you, you may become overly focused on this feeling, thinking it is a fact. You immediately assume they are mad at you because you feel they are mad at you. You will react accordingly, feeling apprehension or fear. However, if you only stop for a minute and consider what facts or reasons your friend may have to be mad at you, you can calmly assess whether or not they are truly upset. In this way, emotional reasoning can cause you unnecessary emotional distress.

Do the above negative thought patterns sound familiar? If they do, then you have traits of self-loathing. But even if that is true, do not worry. This chapter is specifically designed to help you overcome your self-loathing and help you move on to better things.

Before teaching you how to overcome your self-loathing, let's deepen your understanding. Up to this point, you understand self-loathing and what it may look like. This information helps you determine whether or not you are self-loathing and what possible habits you have potentially feeding this trait. Another aspect you must understand is the causes of self-loathing. Knowing where your self-loathing comes from can make you more patient, kind, and compassionate toward yourself. Knowing where a bad habit came from can also be soothing and comforting.

One potential cause of self-loathing is your hostile inner critic. If you remember, many manifestations of self-loathing have to do with your self-criticism and self-judgment, and this is because they feed each other. The more you hate yourself, the harsher your self-criticisms will be. The more powerful your self-criticism, the more you will be convinced you are worthless. Your self-loathing could have started when you began to listen to your negative inner critic more. Once you have succumbed to your hostile inner critic, it would have had free range to ravage your mental health and self-esteem and open the door for self-loathing.

Past traumas may also have sparked your self-loathing. Physical, mental, emotional, sexual, or verbal abuse all qualify as trauma, as do serious car accidents or the sudden loss of loved ones. These traumas, especially at a young age, can imbue you with a sense of regret, self-blame, or shame about what happened. These turbulent emotions can then transform into self-loathing. Suddenly, you hate yourself for not being able to avoid what happened, for causing what happened (this is not true, but it is something you may convince yourself of), for not being able to change your circumstances back then, or for not acting differently. Trauma can keep you locked in the past, and self-loathing can ensure you continue hurting.

Similarly, things from your childhood can build up your self-loathing. For example, suppose your caretakers were critical of you and never acknowledged your achievements. In that case, your self-esteem will be very low as an adult, making you more vulnerable to self-loathing. Another factor from your childhood potentially increasing your risk of self-loathing is the stability and safety of the environment in which you grew up. If you had a very volatile, violent, abusive, or stressful home environment, such as if your parental guardians fought a lot or threatened to leave a lot, then you may have experienced a lot of distress, sadness, worry, and neglect when you were younger. These factors make your negative inner voice a lot louder, thus making you more vulnerable to self-loathing.

Bullying can occur at any age and in any relationship, whether at school, at work, or within personal relationships. A bully would make you feel small, worthless, stupid, and weak. Over time, this will have a lasting impact on how you see yourself. You may internalize the negative messages they say to you and begin to believe you are worthless and weak. If this relates to you,

you must find a way to overcome and face the bullying you experienced. On another note, if you were ever bullied, your self-image may have taken a hit, which would play into your self-loathing. Even though it happened in the past, it affects your self-esteem and self-loathing today. It is best to find ways to deal with it.

Moreover, environmental triggers may remind you of past bullying or traumas. Being reminded of those events can trigger your self-loathing and cause a lot of further emotional distress for you. In certain cases, when you are reminded of past hurts and traumas, your emotional reaction will be huge and out of proportion due to the self-loathing caused by those instances.

Bad relationships are another potential cause of self-loathing because, as with bullying, experiencing this can increase your negative inner voice when you internalize the negative messages sent by the other person. This cause is more damaging than bullying because it is much harder to spot a toxic relationship than to spot bullying. Abusive relationships can be more subtle, and you may even believe the other person is romantic and loving when they are manipulative. As you are blinded to the truth, their abuse increases your hostile inner critic and self-loathing.

Finally, mental health conditions, such as depression or anxiety, can increase your feelings of self-loathing. Some common symptoms of these mental health conditions include self-criticism and self-hate, so it is easy to understand how your self-loathing may be a symptom of an existing mental health condition. Sometimes, even after you have overcome your situation, the habits of self-loathing can linger because you have internalized its messages for some time. You continue feeling hopeless and worthless, but you must continue fighting your self-loathing.

Suppose you do not constantly battle your self-hatred. In that case, there will be severe consequences for your well-being since self-loathing will only grow if it is not addressed. Self-loathing repeatedly tells you that you are not good enough or worthless, and others probably hate you. The effects of believing in these thoughts can be dire. For example, you may begin acting in self-defeating and self-destructive ways by isolating yourself, overreacting, or lashing out at your loved ones. Or you may start relationships with toxic people because you think you deserve the poor treatment they give you. Alternatively, you may find it hard to make decisions independently because you have no trust in your wisdom or discretion, thus increasing your procrastination and preventing you from seizing opportunities in life. You may even hold yourself back from pursuing your goals because you will surely fail. Otherwise, you may develop a depressing outlook on life, have increasingly low self-esteem, or start abusing substances to feel better. All these things will lower your quality of life.

Exercises to Stop Self-Loathing

You must take action to stop your self-loathing tendencies. Easier said than done! Most of the time, you are deeply entrenched in your habit of self-loathing, and breaking away from it seems impossible. You may be used to self-loathing, which looks like it is a natural part of you. But no matter how long you have been having self-loathing thoughts, it does not make it acceptable, natural, or healthy for you to be indulging in them. Self-loathing will only continue to hurt you. You must do what is right for yourself and take any action necessary to stop it.

It can be tough to explore your deepest, darkest thoughts, where they come from, how they affect you, and how you can change them. It requires a lot of mental energy and self-awareness. Some people may find this whole process is made a lot easier with the help of a therapist. A therapist is a licensed and trained mental health professional who has the knowledge, tools, and expertise necessary to help you understand your negative thoughts and replace them with healthier ones. Seeing a therapist is a great way to address and overcome your self-loathing.

There are many functions a therapist can serve. They can act as a guide to help you explore your thoughts because sometimes your inner thoughts are hidden even to yourself. Or a therapist could be like a coach, training you to deal with your negative thoughts and emotions better. Going to therapy could help you find the root cause of your self-loathing and help you develop healthier coping methods to deal with it. You will even be led to create more beneficial traits to replace self-loathing, such as self-compassion and self-love. You may hesitate to see a therapist for your self-loathing because of society's taboo against therapy. But the truth is anyone could benefit from seeing a therapist.

Everyone could use more self-awareness and self-love, which is what treatment can help you achieve. Do not let a fear of judgment stop you from caring for yourself. Also, once you have decided to see a therapist, remember you may need help finding the right therapist. You might have to see a few therapists before finding the one that suits you best. Keep looking, and keep hope!

If you decide therapy is not for you, do not worry. There are countless other exercises you can do to stop self-loathing. One of them is journaling. It can be affirming and cathartic to write down your thoughts. You are releasing them from your head onto a separate, external medium. Try to tell yourself once your thoughts are out of your mind and written on paper, they do not have as much power over you. When they are only vague thoughts in your mind, it is hard to grab hold of them and examine them for truth and logic. But once they are out on paper, you can quickly interrogate them and see your thoughts' accuracy. Plus, you can read through your entries and gain a little perspective when you journal.

Meditating is an excellent accompaniment to journaling, which entails simply sitting with your thoughts and noticing them. Please do not run away from your thoughts, do not hold onto them, and do not react emotionally to them. Allow them to ebb and flow, rise and fall, without being affected by them. Doing this will make you more mindful of your thoughts and more in control of how you want to react to them. It will train you not to respond to the more negative views of your self-loathing.

Self-reflection is another good way to stop your self-loathing. Try to think about where your thoughts are coming from to help treat the root cause rather than the symptom. You were not born with these negative thoughts and attitudes already within you. Something happened to install these negative things in you. Once you realize what exactly caused your self-loathing, you can address the issue. Coming to terms with the initial cause of your self-loathing can significantly reduce the intensity of your self-loathing as its driving force will be gone. When you realize what external factors contribute to your self-loathing, you will understand it more and can remove some of its power.

Next, try to practice self-compassion. Here is a component of self-love that hits two birds with one stone: you will get to train your self-love while also stopping your self-loathing. Self-compassion is a powerful tool against self-loathing as it gears your mind and emotions in precisely the opposite direction compared to self-loathing. While self-loathing condemns and criticizes, self-compassion forgives and understands.

Treating yourself with self-compassion can include telling yourself you are worthy, valuable and deserve to be treated kindly. Over time, you may internalize these messages to replace the negative self-loathing statements. Some practices you can do to treat yourself with self-compassion are to recognize the things you have accomplished, to realize when you are engaged in all-or-nothing thinking, filtering, or emotional reasoning, and to be proactive about changing how you think.

Changing how you think is a tricky thing to do, but it is possible. Now you know the common negative thought patterns of self-loathing, you can be more vigilant in guarding against them and reframing them when you notice them. The next time you catch yourself thinking self-loathing thoughts, try to reframe them and use a slightly different perspective. Challenge yourself to find and accept a middle ground as the truth for all-or-nothing thinking. For filtering, remind yourself of all the positive things about your situation. For emotional reasoning, remind yourself feelings are not facts and challenge yourself to apply more logic and reason to your circumstances. These little changes will slowly reframe your thinking and train your brain to think and react in better, healthier ways.

Try to identify what triggers your self-loathing. Doing this will help you avoid your reaction and calm yourself down. What tends to make you angry at yourself? What were you doing? What did you see? What did you hear? Who were you with? These questions can help you figure out what your triggers are. Once you know them, you will learn to avoid and minimize your reactions to those triggers.

Furthermore, you can stop your self-loathing by talking back to your inner critic. Your inner critic plays a prominent role in self-loathing. If you weaken your inner critic, your self-loathing may also deplete. The next time your inner critic speaks up and starts to tear you down, do not accept whatever it is saying. Stand up for yourself and talk back to it! Ask yourself if your inner critic is being realistic, honest, and fair. Ask yourself if these thoughts are helpful and what benefit you get from them. Then, ask yourself what thoughts may be more effective and productive.

Alternatively, stop self-loathing by practicing self-care. Like self-compassion, self-care is a component of self-love that effectively prevents self-loathing. When you practice self-care, you tell yourself you are someone worth taking care of whose emotional, physical, and psychological needs are essential. Doing this can help you to start loving yourself and stop hating yourself. Some recommendations for self-care to treat self-loathing are to eat healthily, get a good amount of quality sleep, exercise, limit your screen time, take a break from social media, and treat yourself to your favorite food.

If you are a very social person who gains energy from being around people, then an excellent way to combat self-loathing is to surround yourself with positive, optimistic people. Humans tend to mirror the ideas of their communities. When you mix with pessimistic people, you become more susceptible to negative thoughts, such as self-loathing. However, this also means when you mingle with optimistic people, it becomes easier to focus on the good things in life. Reflect on the people in your life. Are any of these people contributing to your self-loathing? Who are you always happy to be around? Who makes you feel more positive about life? Based on these answers, you should have a good idea of the people you want to avoid and the people you should spend more time with. Once you consciously choose to surround yourself with more positive people, you will be happier, more inspired, more motivated, and more optimistic.

Finally, if you are not social but would still like to become more optimistic, you can practice positive self-talk, the opposite of your hostile inner critic. While your negative inner critic has no compassion for you and constantly berates you for any mistakes you make, positive self-talk will treat you with kindness and seek to motivate and comfort you. One way to practice positive self-talk is to list the things you love about yourself or the things you have accomplished that you are proud of. Then, later when you are sinking into self-loathing again, you can read through this list and remind yourself of the good things about yourself. If you cannot think of anything positive to write about yourself, do not worry and do not panic. You have been traversing in self-loathing, and accepting anything positive about yourself is not easy. Give yourself time and keep trying to find things you love about yourself. Eventually, your positive self-talk will get stronger and stronger, enough to combat your hostile inner critic and even your self-loathing.

In this chapter, you have explored self-loathing and how to stop it. These are valuable things to know as you strive toward self-love. You cannot have self-love if you are still holding onto your self-hate; you must slowly let go of self-loathing and leave it behind. One way to do this is to eliminate all the things actively causing your self-hate. Do you remember what one of the more dangerous causes of self-hate is? Yup, toxic relationships. In the next chapter, you will learn how to step away from such relationships and develop healthier ones.

Chapter 3: Building Positive Connections

Self-love is an essential component of any healthy relationship. A lack of self-love can destroy and poison a relationship. Therefore self-love is needed before you enter any relationship. Self-love is essential before entering a relationship because it lets you clearly understand your needs, values, and boundaries. When you love and accept yourself, you are more likely to communicate your needs effectively and make choices in alignment with your values, helping you avoid entering into unhealthy or unfulfilling relationships.

Additionally, self-love can help you be more resilient in the face of relationship challenges and avoid becoming overly dependent on your partner for your sense of self-worth. When you have a strong sense of self-love, you are more likely to enter into a relationship from a place of confidence and self-assurance, which can help create a more balanced and healthy relationship dynamic. Before beginning any relationship, try to ensure you have a good amount of self-love. However, if you are already in a relationship, that is fine too. There are ways to build up self-love, even in a relationship. In addition to learning how to do this, this book will also lead you through how self-love affects friendships, how to walk away from toxic relationships, and how to build more positive ones.

Building Self-Love While in a Relationship

Self-love is a process; you will always have more to learn about and continue developing. There is nothing to say you cannot work on your self-love while already in a relationship. It may be more challenging because you have to focus on the other person as much to ensure their needs are being met. You must also be more aware of how your lack of self-love harms the relationship. But if you remember these two things, you should be able to work on your self-love in a relationship without too much trouble.

First, you can build self-love in a relationship by setting a healthy degree of independence and space. Becoming overly dependent or reliant on the other person is easy when you lack self-love. One way to counteract this is to maintain some distance. Do not let your identity be overthrown by the relationship, and do not allow your values, beliefs, and personality to overshadow your partner's. You are your own person, and you deserve to be yourself. It is best to continue doing your own things, pursuing your interests, and meeting with your friends. However, this is not to say you should neglect your partner. It is only to say you do not need to do everything with them; spending some time apart doing your own thing is healthy.

As an aside, try to remind yourself your partner is not in charge of your happiness. It is not their duty or their responsibility to make you happy. Only you can do that. Your partner can be a great supplement to your happiness, but at the end of the day, they should not be the primary source of it. It is unfair of you to make them responsible for your happiness. It will not be suitable for the relationship either. You will drain them of energy and remove healthy boundaries between you two. Please make sure to charge them with your happiness. You are your own person, and your happiness is your responsibility.

Of course, if you have used them for your happiness, it will be a hard transition, but over time you will get used to it. One way to adopt this new mind frame is to tell yourself your happiness is a choice. It is not something others can give or take away from you. You are in charge of your happiness, which can be hard to accept. Still, once you do, you will be much happier because your happiness will be less affected by the people around you. Your joy will no longer be determined by what is happening around you or by others' opinions of you. When you accept you are in charge of your own happiness, your self-love will grow because you will begin to work on yourself to make yourself happy. Rather than focusing on what others should be doing to provide happiness, you will fulfill yourself by concentrating on what you can do to increase your joy.

Another way to increase your joy and self-love is to be mindful. Sometimes, you are so focused on making yourself happy in the future that you forget how you can be satisfied in the present. You are immersed in everything you are doing to invest in your future happiness, and you stop choosing to be happy right now. Instead of worrying about the future or regretting the past, try to embrace the moment you are currently in. When you are living in the moment, you can do things to increase your happiness, such as following self-care practices.

Often, a lack of self-love can cause you to be insecure and dismiss anything positive others say about you. Sometimes, this can be frustrating and demoralizing for your partner as you refuse to acknowledge all the positive things they see about you. To build self-love, try to see yourself as your partner sees you. The next time they compliment or praise you, do not listen to your automatic reactions to ignore them, insult yourself, or dismiss what they have said. Instead, try to realize this is how they truly feel, and this may be an accurate representation of yourself. You can even start to ask your partner what they love about you, and as they tell you, try to accept this is how they see you.

Over time, you will internalize how they see you and come to see yourself similarly. However, be careful not to use this exercise as an excuse to seek external validation from your partner. You should not ask your partner to list what they love or like about you whenever you feel insecure or when you crave affirmation. Instead, it is best to ask them to accept and internalize their views of you to improve your self-love. If you ask them with these intentions, you will use them as a crutch to support your lack of self-love.

You have learned how you can acknowledge your strengths. But what about your flaws? Self-love applies to both. In relationships, your partner will always appreciate the good parts about you. Still, they also have the right to be irritated at your weaknesses. When they get upset or note your flaws, try not to be disheartened or react negatively. Everyone has imperfections; it is natural for others to notice your weaknesses. If you reflect on yourself, you may realize you get irritated at your partner for their flaws too. The important part is how you deal with the issue now. Some weaknesses can be looked past, and others must be worked on. Either way, having flaws should not make you feel sad or guilty. If you can both work on it and find a healthy way to deal with it, then it is no flaw.

On this note, you must forgive yourself for your mistakes to build up self-love in a relationship. Everyone makes mistakes in relationships. Maybe you forgot an important date or said something in anger you later regretted. Whatever it is, if you refuse to forgive yourself, you will find it increasingly difficult to love yourself. Try to recognize that making mistakes in a relationship is inevitable. Forgiveness would free you to love yourself and your partner more. Of course, you should try to avoid making mistakes and hurting your partner, but when you do, you must know how to forgive yourself and own up to your mistakes.

Lastly, to cultivate more self-love in a relationship, you must realize love is more than a feeling; it is an action. A great way to practice self-love is to act lovingly toward yourself, even if you do not feel too much self-love at the start. Take the time to do self-loving acts to ensure you can teach your mind to love itself. Have some time to yourself every day to practice self-love. It should be your top priority as these actions can significantly increase your self-love. Again, this does not mean you should neglect your partner, but it does mean you must prioritize your needs.

Self-Love and How it Affects Friendships

Self-love also plays an important role in friendships. When you love yourself, you will be more confident and assertive, making establishing and maintaining healthy boundaries in friendships easier. You will also be able to communicate your needs and expectations. All this will allow you to take better care of yourself in any companionship. Not to mention this will encourage your friends to do the same. In this way, you will guide your friends to establish their boundaries with you and communicate their needs and expectations, creating a bond of mutual respect and understanding.

Alongside this, self-love can help you face and overcome the challenges you may experience in your friendships. If you lack self-love, one small bump in the road may be enough to make you give up on the friendship or self-destruct and ruin it. But with healthy levels of self-love, you will have a clearer perspective on things. Namely, you will be less likely to take things too personally. When your friend is having a bad day and lashes out at you, you can stand up for yourself but also empathize with them and understand they are not mad at you or picking on you. They are having an off day. This understanding can prevent small arguments from snowballing into massive conflicts.

Self-love can also improve your relationships with others by making you more empathetic and compassionate. Think about it: Would you rather be close to someone kind, patient, and who can easily understand your experiences, even if they have not been through the same thing, or with someone who focuses more on tough love and who struggles to relate to experiences they have not had before? If you treat others with kindness and care, they will gravitate more toward you. You will be a good listener who understands their concerns, and they will be more inclined to open up to you, increasing your trust.

Since self-love can improve your relationships, a lack of self-love can have the opposite effect. For instance, when you do not have self-love, you may unconsciously choose friends who insult, exploit, or talk down to you. You do this because you believe you deserve this kind of treatment. Or you may apologize too much in your friendships, even when you have not done anything wrong, which will indirectly reinforce to yourself how you should feel guilty for being yourself. These constant messages will decrease your self-esteem and self-love.

A lack of self-love will also harm your friendships because you will not be able to accept praise or compliments from your friends, even when they sincerely try to tell you how they feel. You may indirectly invalidate their feelings and opinions, making them less open to expressing themselves to you. As for how a lack of love may impact your communication skills in friendships, you may begin to see attacks where there are none, and you will become extra defensive during discussions. Unfortunately, this will shut down communication.

If you fall in the latter category where your lack of self-love harms your relationships, here are some valuable tips on how to counteract these effects. Firstly, try not to take things too personally. If there is a difference in views, remember your friend is not necessarily insulting your beliefs. Both of you are entitled to your own opinions. Next, keep yourself from being made small. If you feel like your friend makes you feel bad about yourself, try to bring it up. They may be doing it unintentionally, bringing it up can make them more aware of it. If they are doing it intentionally, then by bringing it up, you will signal to them you will not accept this treatment. Doing this is an excellent way to practice self-love.

How to Walk Away From Toxic Relationships

Toxic relationships can come in many forms, from romantic relationships to friendships and family ties. Whatever the form, you must prepare to walk away from it, especially if it hurts you. Walking away can be tricky—it is never a happy or easy thing to end a relationship—but it is an essential step in your self-love journey.

The first step to walking away from toxic relationships is to recognize when a relationship has gotten toxic. Here are some signs of toxicity in a relationship:

- **It is tiring**: If you are an introvert, spending time with anyone can leave you drained. But spending time with someone toxic, for even an hour, can leave you feeling especially tired and mentally exhausted, introverts and extroverts alike. Notice how you always feel tired after spending time with someone. It is best to be alert to signs of toxicity in the relationship.
- **Overthinking**: If every interaction you have with this person leaves you worried, anxious, fearful, or overthinking about what you may have done wrong or whether or not they are upset with you, then it is a good sign you may need to set up some healthier boundaries.

- **Never apologizing**: If you notice the other person never apologizes to you, no matter how big or small the transgression, and no matter how obvious it is they hurt you or messed up, then you may need to begin considering why it is hard for them to do this. Apologizing is a sign of humility, of embracing and learning from mistakes. If this person cannot do this, it shows they are unwilling to take responsibility for hurting you, which is a sign of a toxic relationship.

- **No support**: If the other person does not want you to succeed or be happy, it is probably an unhealthy relationship. In positive and healthy relationships you will wish for each other to flourish and grow. Even in neutral relationships with people you are not close to; there is no hatred or ill will. You can both go about your lives and not be affected much by the success or failure of the other. But in toxic relationships, things can get competitive, which can warp any good things happening to you. If you do not feel encouraged or supported, it is time to ask why the other person does not like seeing you succeed.

- **Controlling behaviors**: Every relationship comprises two individuals with their own opinions and free will. You may affect each other's habits and thoughts because of how well you get along. Still, suppose the other person ever tries to change or control you against your will. In that case, it is a sign to re-examine the relationship. Some common controlling behaviors include demanding updates on your whereabouts, getting angry at you if you do not reply to them fast enough, or stopping you from hanging out with certain people. There are many reasons why someone may exhibit controlling behaviors. Still, the result is an unhealthy relationship with the potential to cause you harm. It is best to learn to stand up for yourself.

Once you realize you are in an unhealthy relationship, the second step is to prioritize your safety, happiness, and well-being. If a relationship fits the above criteria, then the relationship may not be suitable for you. Tell yourself and try to accept you deserve to be treated with kindness and respect. Then, try to take action to ensure this happens. This action can come in various forms, such as:

- **Communicating your needs**: Be honest and tell the person how they affect you. They may not mean to hurt you, and once you make them more aware, they will try to change their behavior. While you are communicating your needs to them, make sure to be assertive. Do not back down from your points; let them know how you have been feeling and what changes you want to occur. In the best-case scenario, they accept, apologize, and try to make a change. Worst case scenario, you realize they do not intend to change, and you must make the necessary decision to take care of yourself.
- **Making a plan**: Once you decide you need to leave, there are a few necessary steps. For example, start to limit your contact with the other person, set healthy boundaries and enforce them, or cut ties with the person altogether.
- **Seeking support**: When you decide to end a relationship, it is a hard step and a complex process. You must create a support system to offer you emotional support and practical help during this trying time. You may need to seek out trusted friends, relatives, or even a therapist.

Walking away from an unhealthy relationship is hard but worth it. The benefits it will have for your self-love are essential. When you stay in a toxic relationship, you are not valuing yourself, which will affect your self-esteem, self-worth, and self-love. Walking away from unhealthy relationships is a massive step in the right direction, as you tell yourself you deserve better and to be treated with respect and love. The first benefit is your self-love will increase. Other benefits include the improvement of your mental and emotional well-being. Toxic relationships can strain your mind as you are always scared or apprehensive of how the other person is feeling or what they may do or say to you.

When you walk away, you remove this element from your life, and you will experience a sense of relief and calm. Finally, walking away from a bad relationship can open you up to spending more time and energy in your positive relationships, helping you further create a fulfilling and happy life.

Building Positive Relationships

Now you know how to walk away from unhealthy relationships, it is time you learn how to build positive ones. It is not enough to cut out the weeds from your garden; you must also begin to plant some flowers. Doing this will help develop self-love in the long run because positive relationships will keep you optimistic and happy. And this will then make you more inclined to treat yourself with love and kindness.

The first tip on how to build positive relationships is to keep expectations realistic. Do not impose your values and ideals onto others because it is not their responsibility to live up to your expectations. No one is perfect, and you should not expect them to be, especially not by your personal, subjective expectations. A healthy relationship involves accepting someone for who they are and not trying to change them.

Communication is vital in building a healthy relationship too. A lack of self-love is one of the reasons why communication falls apart in relationships. Now you have more self-love, healthy communication has become available to you. There are many aspects to healthy communication, including:

- giving each other time to express yourselves
- being mindful and present (that is, not distracted)
- actively listening
- trying to empathize with what they are feeling
- asking questions to clarify their meaning
- maintaining eye contact to show you are engaged
- being open and honest with each other

Otherwise, try to be flexible in your relationships. A lot of relationships break because one person refuses to bend. It is unnatural for a relationship to remain the same forever. It is natural for things to change and grow, do not try to run away from change. Embrace and accept it; this is how you can nurture the relationship.

Suppose you are the type of person who always tries to care for others and often neglects themselves. In that case, you must be mindful of this in your relationships and stop yourself from ignoring your needs. You must take care of yourself and give your partner space to express your needs.

This next point may seem like it is not worth mentioning. Still, you would be surprised how many overlook it: Being dependable in relationships is essential. If you have made a commitment, you must honor it, and this will build up mutual trust.

If there are ever any conflicts in your relationships, you must know how to handle them. The first thing to do is to make sure you never discuss things while you are still angry; this is a surefire way to say something you may regret. Instead, calm down before you initiate a discussion to open the door for more productive and respectful conversations. Then, while expressing yourself, try to use more "I" statements rather than "You" statements. The latter tends to assign blame and raise the other person's defenses. For example, "You made me feel like this." Whereas the former focuses on your emotions without assuming the other person's intentions. For example, "I felt like this when you said this." Using "I" statements can keep the other person open to listening to you.

Some other strategies for conflict resolution are to keep your language clear and specific. If you are clear about how you feel or what the issue is, then it is easier to address the problem, and there are less chances for misunderstandings. Next, attack the issue at hand, do not attack the person. If you start to attack the person personally, their defenses will rise, and communication will shut down. Not to mention the actual problem will not be addressed.

Some final strategies to build positive relationships are to be affirming, balanced, and be yourself! When you confirm, the other person will feel cared for and validated, encouraging them to be more open and honest with you, thus deepening the relationship. When you are balanced, you ensure you are not overly reliant on any one person and are taking care of your own needs, which can increase your self-confidence and self-love. Finally, when you are yourself, you are being true to yourself, and this will improve your self-esteem. Plus, healthy relationships can only occur when you are being your true self and letting yourself be seen by others.

A lack of positive relationships can negatively affect your life in many ways. One of the effects is you will be more susceptible to symptoms of depression. Of course, there are many other possible reasons why you may be dealing with depression. In the next chapter, you will explore the relationship between self-love and depression and the tools you can use to overcome this issue.

Chapter 4: Telling Depression to F*** Off

In the previous chapter, you looked at the relationships you have in your life, potentially hindering your self-love. However, your relationship with yourself is essential to your self-love journey. A common ailment in your relationship with yourself is depression. This mental illness can significantly steal the joy from your life and ruin your relationship with yourself by feeding you lies, criticisms, and judgments about yourself. The next step in your self-love journey is to learn to tell depression to f*** off!

Clinical depression is a mental condition affecting your daily life. Still, clinical depression can be effectively treated through therapy, medication, and lifestyle changes. If you are concerned you have depression, do not worry because there are various strategies you can use to combat this illness! This chapter will focus on the lifestyle changes and exercises you can do to treat your symptoms. These exercises can be incredibly uplifting and helpful. However, you can always use these valuable strategies in tandem with therapy. They are trained to help people in your exact situation. If you are having trouble managing your symptoms of depression even with the exercises given here, then perhaps you would benefit more from seeing a mental health professional. Keep this option in mind as you move forward.

There are many types of depression you may be struggling with. To help you understand your condition better, let's briefly go through the possible disorders you may be facing. Firstly, there is major depressive disorder, the most common form of depression. Its symptoms include anxious distress, melancholy, weight loss, suicidal thoughts, or agitation. These symptoms must be present for two weeks or more to be diagnosed with this disorder. If the symptoms last for at least two years, then it can be said that you have a persistent depressive disorder.

Another form of depression is bipolar disorder; you swing between manic episodes (where you are high-energy and impulsive) and depressive episodes (where you are low-energy and feel hopeless). You could also be facing seasonal affective disorder, where you experience symptoms of depression due to the effects of your surroundings, specifically the seasons. Most people experience this disorder during winter when there is less sunlight, and it is generally more gloomy. However, there are a few rare cases where this disorder is also experienced in the spring and summer.

Psychotic depression is a more extreme form of depression where you experience psychotic symptoms like hallucinations, delusions, or paranoia. Or you may be dealing with atypical depression, where a positive event can elevate your mood for a while. If this is the case, it means your symptoms of depression are not as consistent or persistent as other forms of depression.

Treatment-resistant depression is another form of depression, and its name is self-explanatory. People with this disorder may go through several treatment options with meager success rates. However, because your condition is resistant to treatment does not mean it is impossible to treat. There are still many strategies and unconventional treatment methods you can try.

Suppose you are a woman who has given birth. In that case, it is even possible you have postpartum depression; typically something experienced a few weeks and months after childbirth. Another form of depression specific to women is premenstrual dysphoric disorder, which is the depression you may feel right before your period starts. The symptoms include mood swings, anxiety, fatigue, or feeling overwhelmed.

These are all the possible forms of depression you may be experiencing. All these different forms have various possible causes and treatments. Self-love is an exciting factor in depression because a lack of it can worsen your symptoms, while an increase in self-love can help treat your symptoms. There are many ways self-love and depression can interact; let's explore their relationship now.

The Relationship Between Self-Love and Depression

Self-love can significantly affect how you feel about yourself, which is vital when dealing with depression. When you do not have self-love, you may suffer from low self-esteem, low self-confidence, and low self-worth, all of which will heighten your symptoms of depression and lower your mood. However, it is not a clear cause-and-effect relationship. Your symptoms of depression and your self-love interact with each other and affect one another. When you practice more self-love, your symptoms of depression will be alleviated and less severe. When your symptoms of depression worsen, it becomes harder to practice self-love, and your thoughts about yourself will become more negative. It is a two-way street where both elements can influence each other.

For your specific case, as you strive to improve your self-love, it is crucial to understand how self-love can influence depression because it can emphasize to you how your self-love may further benefit your mental health and help you stay vigilant against symptoms of depression. It has been well established how low levels of self-love and self-esteem can increase your risk of mental health problems. One study on this topic even showed how participants who reported low levels of self-love and self-esteem were almost six times more likely to develop depression and four times more likely to have experienced some symptoms of depression than other participants (Kolonko, 2022). Meaning the more self-love you have, the less likely you are to develop depression or to experience symptoms of depression. Whether you have a depressive disorder or are worried about creating one, self-love can help improve your mental health and keep depression far away.

Taking a closer look into how self-love affects depression, it is vital to understand how a lack of self-love can change your outlook on life. When you do not love yourself, you are more likely to engage in self-destructive behaviors and to have negative thoughts and feelings about yourself. This way, you can drown in negativity, making you more likely to develop depression. When you have low self-love, you will not think much of yourself. Thus you may often look down on yourself or blame yourself for things that are not your fault, creating a heavy sense of guilt and weighing on every part of your life. You may feel guilty for not being good enough, letting people down, or making small mistakes. You may blame yourself whenever anything wrong happens and feel guilty about it, even if you have nothing to do with it. This immense guilt can lead you to hopelessness and eventually depression. Once you develop symptoms of depression, you may begin to feel guilty about those symptoms. It is an endless cycle of negativity. The good thing is you can remove yourself from this dark cycle by simply practicing more self-love. Do not allow yourself to get caught up by the harms of low self-love. Instead, open yourself up to the benefits of loving yourself more!

Next, how does depression affect self-love? Suppose you have ever had a depressive episode or experienced symptoms of depression. In that case, you know it usually feels impossible to be loving to yourself during those times. However, because it feels impossible does not mean it is. It will be harder to practice self-love when you are feeling depressed, but your mental health will thank you if you do. But coming back to how depression affects self-love, why is it hard to practice it when you are depressed?

One possible reason is the symptoms of depression are much the same as the effects you experience when you have low levels of self-love. You will feel inferior, worthless, and unconfident when you do not love yourself. Similarly, during a depressive episode, your self-esteem will plummet, and you will have more self-critical and self-deprecating thoughts, often preventing you from feeling any love for yourself.

Another reason is being depressed can damage your ability to perform, achieve, or even try. When symptoms of depression bog you down, it can be hard to leave your bed, let alone win a big competition or continue training for something. When you are not achieving or actively working toward a goal, it can be harder to feel proud of yourself and love yourself. Depression also makes it harder to love yourself by increasing your feelings of hopelessness. A common symptom of depression is hopelessness; when you feel like this, you will have a negative outlook on yourself and your future. You will switch out your lens of self-love for the lens of pessimism and criticism.

Moreover, when you are experiencing depression, you may develop a negative self-image, higher self-criticism, and more self-doubt about your abilities and personality, making it harder for you to accept compliments and positive feedback from others. When you cannot believe anything positive about yourself, it gets much harder to practice self-love.

In summary, self-love and depression are closely related and constantly affect one another. A lack of self-love can contribute to the development of depression. In contrast, depression can make it harder to practice self-love. If you are struggling with depression, you need to work on developing your self-love, as it can be a powerful tool in the recovery process. It is also important to seek help from a therapist or counselor if you are struggling with depression and need additional support. Therapists can hold your hand and guide you through the healing process. In the meantime, something you can do for yourself to help kick depression's a** is to learn how to accept positivity from others.

Accepting Positivity From Others

As you have observed, it is hard to practice self-love when feeling depressed. Negative thoughts and emotions will constantly be assailing you. You may not have the energy or mental space to even think about practicing self-love. That is okay. It is not an easy feat. In the beginning, try to focus more on accepting love from others rather than practicing self-love. If you cannot find love within yourself, try to find it in others. Of course, this is not a lifestyle you should always practice. It is a temporary salve to help you during your depressive episodes. To be clear, you should not make it a habit to seek external validation or depend on external sources to feel love for yourself because this is not a healthy or sustainable path to self-love. However, when you are depressed, you can use these methods to prevent yourself from spiraling into a deeper state of depression. Then, once you have elevated your mood and cleared your mind, you can practice self-love again. But to get to this state, you must first rely on your loved ones to remind you and affirm that you are lovable and valuable.

When you do not see yourself in a positive light and do not believe in your skills and abilities, it can be tough to accept and believe others see you positively. Even then, it can be hard to believe what they are telling you and internalize their positive messages. It is hard to accept positivity from others when you are feeling depressed because your self-esteem and self-confidence would have plummeted drastically.

You may compare their positive messages with your highly negative image of yourself and then decide to dismiss all the loving messages they have said and tell yourself they cannot possibly be telling the truth. You may convince yourself they are not being sincere or trying to deceive you. Even in cases where you believe they are being genuine, you may still feel uncomfortable accepting their praise. When this happens, you may downplay yourself or ignore what they have said. Hearing good things about yourself when you are depressed can be uncomfortable because it does not align with the current thoughts and emotions tearing you down. When you are confronted by things disagreeing with your inner voice and self-narration, you may feel very aversive. You may feel like you do not deserve their praise. Or you may even feel guilty as you have tricked them into believing you are a good person when you are not.

There are countless ways in which you may dismiss or ignore loving messages when you're feeling depressed. However, it is important not to give in to this. Try your best to accept the positivity others are offering you. This can help you regain your mental footing and begin practicing self-love again. Think of it as a stepping stone to self-love. It may be too big of a jump to start practicing self-love when feeling depressed. Take baby steps instead. Start by accepting the love of others to bring you one step closer to practicing self-love on your own again.

So how can you start accepting positivity from others? The first step is to recognize the negative thoughts preventing you from accepting them. Usually, when someone says something kind about you, your negative thoughts may automatically flare up to counteract the kindness with pessimism and criticism. Your mind may begin talking down to you and insulting your abilities and personality. Try to catch yourself when you are doing this and tell yourself these thoughts have nothing to do with what the other person said. Those thoughts do not change the kindness you have been given. Rather than wasting your energy on those pointless thoughts, try to accept kindness for what it is.

Next, try to practice self-compassion. Accepting positivity from others can increase your self-compassion. Self-compassion entails treating yourself like you would treat your friends, forgiving yourself when you mess up, and being understanding rather than judgmental. When you can treat yourself this way, accepting the love others give you will feel more natural. Your self-love will begin to mend as well. However, there are times when your symptoms of depression may spiral out of control. In these instances, it can be hard to practice self-compassion or to focus on anything other than the intense negativity you feel. When you are faced with cases like this, an excellent strategy to combat depression and regain your self-love is to seek professional help. Going to therapy can help you gain a better perspective of your situation. You will also be led to consider, challenge, and replace the negative thoughts and beliefs currently making it hard for you to accept positivity from others.

It is best also to practice gratitude. When you take the time to appreciate all the positive things in your life, you gear your mind to being more receptive to positivity, thus allowing the love and kindness of others to penetrate more easily into your consciousness. The next time someone compliments you, try acknowledging and accepting their kind words rather than deflecting or ignoring them. As you are doing this, being patient with yourself is essential. Remember, it is no easy feat to deal with depression, and these habits of rejecting positivity have probably been ingrained in you for some time. It is going to take some time and effort to learn new, healthier habits. Be patient with yourself and give yourself credit for all the actions you have taken and the progress you have made.

Finally, learn to recognize the positive attributes you have. Look at what positive traits you have, your talents, and your achievements. Remind yourself you have positive qualities which should be commended. You may not immediately feel better after doing this. Still, at least all your positive points will be raised to your awareness, making it harder to reject or ignore them when others notice them too. Accepting positivity from others is a process, and it takes time and effort to change your negative thoughts and beliefs. With the right mindset, self-compassion, and support, it is possible to learn to accept positivity and return to self-love.

Exercises to Treat Symptoms of Depression

Other than learning to accept positivity from others, you can do countless other exercises to treat your symptoms of depression. Firstly, there is mindfulness meditation, which requires you to focus on the present moment instead of worrying about the future or regretting the past. To do this exercise, try to sit in a comfortable position and focus on breathing to ground you in the present moment. As you are focusing, try to notice your thoughts and emotions. Allow them to come and go, do not chase, ignore, or hold onto any of them. Instead, try to let them occur without being affected by them. In this way, you become aware of your thoughts and emotions without judging them and without being harmed by them. When you can observe your thoughts and feelings without being influenced by them, you can significantly reduce your symptoms of depression and improve your mental health.

Besides mindfulness meditation, you can change your lifestyle by exercising more. Physical activity can do wonders for your mental health. Biologically, exercise can initiate the release of endorphins or happy hormones that help you deal with stress, reduce your pain, and make you feel satisfied. Mentally, exercise can allow you to work out any tension and help you feel good about your body. Exercise can also be a form of self-expression as you move your body freely, usually insignificant, unreserved movements. All this can reduce your symptoms of depression while also improving your physical health.

One specific type of exercise often used these days to combat depression is yoga. This exercise can be combined with mindfulness meditation, where you try to be present while doing various yoga poses. Even on its own, yoga can reduce stress, calm your mind, raise your self-awareness, and help you achieve a more peaceful state of mind. Therefore, this will help reduce your depression symptoms and increase your self-love.

Something else you could incorporate into your lifestyle is journaling. This great habit allows you to write down your thoughts and emotions. There are many benefits to doing this. For one, it can be validating and cathartic. When you write down what you are thinking, it is almost as if you are accepting this is how you feel and telling yourself it is okay to feel this way. If you are feeling overwhelmed by your thoughts and emotions, writing them down can be a way of getting those tumultuous feelings out of your mind and onto paper. Doing this can help you deal with those emotions better. Another benefit to journaling is you get to go back and reread what you have written. You can better understand what you are feeling, and it helps you reflect and process your thoughts. Journaling can provide you with clarity and perspective on various situations.

One specific form of journaling you could benefit from is gratitude journaling. Here you have a type of journal specifically meant to increase your gratitude and give you a space to remember all the positive things in your life. To do this exercise, write down what you are grateful for today. Gratitude journaling is usually done at night, right before you sleep, to ensure you can reflect on an entire day. As you are remembering, look for positive parts of your day, then write down what happened and why you are grateful for it. Doing this can improve your mood, remind you to stay optimistic, and increase your general well-being.

Journaling is something you can do on your own to help combat depression. But if you are more of an extroverted and social person, then you can rely on social support to help you battle your symptoms. If you have a proper support system, do not be afraid to rely on them. The positive relationships you have with others can remind you you are a person of value with people around you who care about you. Plus, spending time with those you are close to is like a natural mood booster. Suppose you are feeling especially down in the dumps. In that case, your friends and family can even be there to comfort you and help you get through this depressive episode.

Cognitive behavioral therapy (CBT) is another strategy to treat your depression symptoms. CBT is often done with the help of a therapist. Still, you can try to do it on your own —as long as you properly educate yourself first and ensure you can conduct this treatment responsibly and effectively. If you are unsure about it, it is best to get the help of a mental health professional. CBT can help you identify, challenge, and replace negative thought patterns, habits, and coping mechanisms. It can help you start accepting positivity from others by challenging the thoughts maintaining your depression, and it will increase your levels of self-love. Of course, every case of depression is unique, and your battle with mental health and depression will warrant specific strategies and methods of CBT. What works for you with CBT may not work for another person; it is on a case-by-case basis. Suppose you are having trouble figuring out how to benefit from CBT. In that case, it may be best for you to consult a therapist and work with them to find the best approach.

Yet another lifestyle change you can try is to schedule your life more. Depression can throw a wrench into your usual routine. It can make it harder for you to wake up in the morning or honor your commitments. Try to counteract these effects by making a schedule to help you get back on track and slowly return to normal. In relation to this, try to set goals for yourself. These do not have to be long-term goals or highly ambitious goals. Set a few things you want to accomplish for the day. When you succeed at this, you will feel better about yourself, making it easier to start practicing self-love again and reduce your symptoms of depression.

These are all way you can tell depression to f*** off. Do not forget that self-love is a powerful tool against depression. Keep increasing your self-love, and the rest will follow! Up next, you will learn how self-love can improve your self-image.

Chapter 5: Loving Your Self-Image and Your Body

When you practice self-love, this applies to every part of yourself. You cannot be loving to yourself if you hate or reject parts of yourself. It is essential to include your physical body in your self-love. For many people, their body image causes a snag in their self-love. They may be able to accept their weaknesses and commend their accomplishments. Still, they cannot say anything good about their physical body. Behavior like this is worrying because self-love should be all-encompassing, including your body. How can you say you love yourself if you do not accept parts of your physical body?

When you do not accept your body, this can cause a lot of issues in your life. The self-rejection and self-denial caused by this will lower your self-esteem and self-confidence, thus making it harder to love yourself. You may also use unhealthy coping mechanisms to deal with your negative body image. For example, you may exercise excessively, eat too little, or start to abuse substances. It is okay to want to improve your physical health and physique as long as you can still accept your current body. If you cannot do this, then it will be hard for you to practice self-love. To help you start loving yourself—body included—you will explore what self-image and body image entail, why you may be insecure about your body, and how to begin accepting and loving your body.

What Are Self-Image and Body Image?

How well you love your body and yourself is affected by two key elements: self-image and body image. Self-image has to do with your mental photo of yourself, including your personality, traits, strengths, and weaknesses. Self-image is a more general picture of how you view yourself. At the same time, body image zooms into how you view your physical body. Ask yourself what type of person you are and how you would describe yourself. The answer to this question makes up your self-image.

So how did you develop this way of seeing yourself? Many factors influence your self-image, but a significant factor is your early childhood influences. When you are young, you do not have much of a self-concept yet, and you may be unsure how to view yourself. You look to the opinions of others, typically people of authority who you trust, to inform you about yourself. You may observe the opinions of your parents, older siblings, teachers, or peers and internalize their opinions to create your self-image. If your parents always praised you, this would have improved your self-image and helped you see yourself positively. If your friends or siblings were constantly insulting you and picking on your mistakes, this would have harmed your self-image and made you see yourself more negatively. These effects may have carried on into your adulthood, and the type of self-image you have now may have been significantly affected by your early childhood influences.

Your current relationships in adulthood can also continue affecting your self-image. Suppose you surround yourself with people who acknowledge your accomplishments and compliment and treat you kindly. In that case, you will enjoy a healthy self-image. You may see yourself as they see you and thus believe you are a successful, worthwhile person who deserves to be treated nicely. On the flip side, if you surround yourself with people who talk down to you and minimize your achievements, then you may begin to see yourself as a failure who does not deserve to be treated with respect. Do you see how your self-image can get distorted? When you start listening to the negative opinions of others, you may become less able to see yourself realistically, developing a pessimistic self-image. All in all, your relationships with others can reinforce or influence how you see yourself. It is best to surround yourself with good people who make you feel better about yourself.

An awareness of your strengths and weaknesses can affect your self-image too. Who you are is not a constant, unchanging thing. You are constantly changing, growing, adapting, and learning, meaning your strengths and weaknesses will change over time. As you navigate life, you may gain more skills, forget some skills, eliminate flaws, realize new weaknesses, or even enhance specific strengths.

Something that made you feel good or bad about yourself in the past may not hold in the future, making it integral to practice self-awareness to ensure you always have a realistic and balanced self-image. Knowing your strengths and weaknesses can affect how you think about yourself and how you act. Hopefully, you can develop a healthy self-image where you can admire and recognize your strengths while being realistic and accepting of your weaknesses. A negative self-image would create a distorted view where you overly focus on your weaknesses, catastrophize your flaws, and ignore your strengths.

Your self-image is important because it dictates how you think about yourself, feel about yourself, and interact with others in life. When you have a positive self-image, you will feel good about yourself, be able to think about yourself in realistic, fair, and compassionate terms, and interact with others in an open and friendly way. When you have a negative self-image, you will feel bad about yourself, only think about yourself in cruel, unrealistic, and judgmental terms, and only interact with others in insecure and unhealthy ways. Suppose you want to care for your physical, mental, emotional, and social well-being. In that case, you must develop a healthy self-image. The promising news is that self-image is not a constant thing. As mentioned already, your self-image is constantly changing.

Now, you need to direct the change actively. Some strategies to do this are to list your strengths, make realistic and achievable goals, explore your early childhood influences, stop comparing yourself to others, positively affirm yourself every morning, and remember you are a unique and worthy person. Try to challenge your negative self-image and create a more accurate way of viewing yourself.

A specific aspect of self-image often hinders people from self-love is body image. This aspect is being concerned with what you look like and how you think others see you. While self-image has to do with your qualities, traits, skills, and personality, body image focuses primarily on your physical looks and how you feel and think about your body.

Many factors, such as societal beauty standards and cultural ideas, can affect your body image. These standards and images fill your mind with messages about beauty and how you should strive to look. These messages are detrimental because they often only endorse one specific type of beauty and do not account for various body types, creating an unrealistic expectation and standard for you which is almost impossible to attain. When you buy into society's or culture's beauty standards, your body image may deteriorate as you constantly chase an unrealistic ideal of perfection.

Your body image also may be influenced by your family and the things they say about your body. Everybody has relatives who say whatever they are thinking without any filter. They may comment on your body and enforce their beauty standards onto you without consideration. Try to ignore them and not be affected by what they say; it still hurts to have negative comments thrown at you, especially in front of others. The negative comments of family or friends can chip away at your body image.

Finally, a significant contributor to a negative body image is the habit of comparison. Do you have someone you are constantly comparing yourself to physically? You may want to be as tall as them, as thin as them, as pretty as they are, or as strong as they are. But you must realize that, as long as you are comparing yourself to others, you will never feel good enough. There will always be someone you will compare yourself to and feel bad about yourself. Rather than constantly comparing yourself, try to tell yourself everyone's body is different. Focus on your body to improve what you can and accept what you cannot.

Body image is a vital part of self-image. When you have a positive body image, you will feel comfortable in your skin and confident in yourself. When you have a negative body image, it is almost as if you are rejecting yourself. Soaking in feelings like this will cause you a lot of mental anguish and discomfort.

How can you improve your body image? Well, the first thing you must do is change how you think and feel about your body. To do this:

1. Try to realistically assess your physical body and your common thoughts about it.
2. Try to find any distortions in your thoughts which may be harming you.
3. Once you identify them, challenge them and tell yourself your thoughts are inaccurate representations of reality. Once you can see yourself more realistically, you will recognize what you can and cannot change about yourself.

As you develop a healthier relationship with your body, you can begin transforming your body itself. If you tried to change your body before you had a healthy relationship with it, you probably would have used extreme and unkind methods to change yourself. You must learn to accept and love your body before you try to change it.

Where Do Insecurities Come From?

A prevalent symptom of poor self-image and body image is insecurities. When you do not see yourself or your body in a positive light, you will be wracked with insecurities resulting in lower self-confidence and keeping you from self-love. However, once you know where your insecurities are coming from, you can actively try to counteract those effects or avoid those triggers. Let's explore all the different things which could heighten your insecurities.

Firstly, there is the pressure you feel from the media. Media can be anything from movies, television shows, magazines, music, and social media. These outlets usually project an ideal image for you to chase and emulate. And if you do not live up to those standards, you may begin to feel insecure about yourself. The most common platform to perpetuate these standards is social media. It is easy to start comparing yourself to those you see online. You may look at someone's picture and compare your body to theirs. Or you may see someone's post about their accomplishments and feel bad about your achievements. If you interact with it this way, social media can harm your self-image and body image. A way to avoid this is to stop comparing yourself to others. You can compliment others on their beauty or skills, but remember you have unique strengths you should be proud of.

Insecurities can also come from a place of low self-esteem. As you know, self-esteem relates to how much you believe in your abilities and worth. When you have low self-esteem, you will not have confidence in yourself, leading to more insecurities. Many things can cause low self-esteem. If you were bullied in the past or were a victim or witness to abuse, you are more likely to have low self-esteem as an adult. Various mental health conditions may also lead you to develop low self-esteem. The people you spend time with can also affect your self-esteem if they always put you down or make fun of you. Insecurities are not naturally occurring things. They are something you learn. Do not let those around you teach you to have low self-esteem. Instead, surround yourself with more positive and kind people.

It is also worth noting that if you have an eating disorder, you may suffer from very poor self-image, particularly your body image. A major symptom of eating disorders is a distorted view of your physical body. You may think your body is too big, even within the healthy weight range. You may have internalized unhealthy and unrealistic beauty standards, driving your poor body image. These standards can lead you to have deep fears about food, eating, weight gain, and social judgment. You will be overly focused on your body and its perceived flaws, creating a negative headspace, eventually leaking into other areas of your life.

You may also become more insecure due to specific events or experiences. For example, if you recently suffered a failure or rejection, your insecurities may be high. Your life experiences can define you and influence how you see yourself. They can also dictate your mood. For example, if you recently scored well on an exam you placed a lot of emphasis on, you will find it easier to see yourself as intelligent, successful, and capable. You will then be in a good mood. However, suppose you recently got reprimanded by your boss for the quality of your work. In that case, you may find it difficult to see yourself positively. Instead, all your insecurities, which were lying dormant, may awaken and begin screaming in your mind. You may use this experience to reinforce yourself that you are a failure, unskilled, or incapable of holding down a job. All these negative thoughts about yourself will put you in a more downcast disposition. The events in your life can significantly affect your confidence, insecurities, and mood. It is easy to feel happy and confident when good things keep happening in your life. But when bad things happen, you quickly get lost in your insecurities.

A mindset you can use to help yourself stay happy and confident despite the negative events in your life is to remind yourself life has its ups and downs; it cannot be perfect all the time. You are in a lull, a down, but pretty soon, life will pick itself back up again. Be sure to persevere through the various setbacks you may face in life. Negative events, failure, and rejection are bound to happen at some point in life, so you should stay happy through it all rather than become discouraged and hopeless.

You may also have to deal with more insecurities if you have social anxiety. Social anxiety is a mental disorder in which you are terrified of being humiliated in public or judged negatively by others. Almost everyone has felt nervous in social settings before. It is pretty ordinary. Most family gatherings, dates, interviews, or parties can make you overthink and feel a bit stressed. However, people with social anxiety may feel paralyzed by this fear and anxiety. They find the possibility of humiliation or judgment in social settings to be debilitating. Due to these fears, you may become extra aware of your flaws, imperfections, and mistakes because, in your mind, these are all things with the potential to embarrass you or cause others to criticize you. You may become more insecure about yourself, your looks, and your actions. All this will harm your self-image and body image. You may even begin avoiding social situations to prevent those feelings of fear, anxiety, and insecurity.

Finally, your insecurity may be coming from your perfectionism. Perfectionism is a trait where you want everything to be flawless, or you want to be viewed by others as being perfect. Perfectionism causes you to have high standards for yourself and be highly critical of yourself. Nothing is ever good enough, and something is always stopping things from being perfect. With this mindset, it's easy to see why you may be more insecure. You will be your worst critic, always picking on the small mistakes you made and talking down to yourself for not being perfect.

Exercises to Improve Self-Love and Body Acceptance

Now that you understand more about self-image, body image, and insecurities let's dive into exercises to help overcome any insecurities and increase our self-love, confidence, and esteem.

The first step is to improve your self-love and body acceptance. To do this, try to become more aware of the words you use to talk to yourself and the messages you send yourself. When you speak to yourself, are you being kind or cruel? Accepting and loving yourself is tough if you are being cruel to yourself. Try to catch yourself when criticizing or judging yourself, and replace those words and messages with something kinder and more constructive. Most times, your negative statements are not helpful at all. Try to change them into positive messages to address your issues and focus on the solution instead.

The next step is to remind yourself self-love is a skill, an act, and a choice. Self-love does not simply happen. It needs time and effort, and it is a conscious choice for you to practice it, meaning no amount of external positivity will be able to create self-love for you. No matter how many people love you and praise you, how many promotions you get, and how happy you are in your relationship, you will not achieve self-love unless you are actively trying to cultivate it. Self-love will not eventually hit you from the outside and will not suddenly happen on the inside. Stop waiting for self-love to happen to you, and stop thinking self-love will come with a specific set of circumstances (such as once you reach a certain weight or get rid of certain imperfections). It is up to you to make self-love happen.

To focus more on your body image, you should notice where your relationship with your body is expressing itself. When you have a negative association with your body, this will show. It will physically manifest itself somewhere, and you must be aware of it. For example, you may think you are too overweight and thus begin to limit the food you give yourself. Restricting eating is worrying as you may deny your body the nutrients it needs to function.

On the other hand, you may think you are too skinny and overwork yourself at the gym, which could lead to injuries and other physical ailments. There are many different ways your negative body image may manifest itself; pay attention to your habits and actions. Ask yourself your motivations and try to get to the bottom of what you need.

Insecurities and negative self-image can be interpreted as symptoms of depression. Understandably, some treatments for depression can effectively treat your insecurities and raise your body's acceptance. On this note, mindfulness meditation is a great way to combat negative self-image. Your negative thoughts about your body and yourself may be spontaneous and automatic. You may not even realize you are thinking this way.

Mindfulness meditation can make you more aware of these thoughts, which is the first step to changing them. This form of meditation can also reduce the harmful effects of these thoughts on you. You will train yourself not to react to those thoughts, instead allowing them to pass you. You can even use mindfulness meditation to increase your self-love by including positive affirmations, such as "I love my body" or "I am a good person," as you meditate.

You can remind yourself that you are not alone in your battle against insecurities and negative self-image. Often, you can be focused on your problems and struggles, and you forget to zoom out and realize many other people are dealing with the same issue. For example, if you are worried others are judging you, and you feel insecure because of this, try to empathize with others. They are probably not focused on you but on their issues and insecurities instead! Remember, insecurities are a universal human experience. If you are not wasting your time judging others for their flaws, others probably are not doing this to you.

Insecurities and negative self-image can make you overly focused on judgment—the personal critiques you have against yourself and the possible judgments others may be thinking. If you have noticed a flaw or a mistake, judging yourself will only make you feel worse. You may begin to obsess over the little mistake, freeze, and ultimately break down, which is not helpful. To break out of this pattern, try to practice self-kindness instead. Rather than self-destructing, a little self-kindness can go a long way. When you treat yourself with kindness in the face of mistakes, you remind yourself it is okay to make mistakes, making it easier for you to learn from your mistakes and bounce back.

Some extra tips for you are to use positive affirmations to encourage and comfort yourself. Write down positive messages about yourself, your body, and your abilities. You may not immediately believe in these messages, but the main point is they have to be positive. Then, repeat these affirmations to yourself every day. Though you may not believe what you are saying, you will eventually internalize those messages and start trusting in them. It is best to practice more self-care because this will reinforce that you are someone of worth and you matter. It will increase your self-esteem and reduce your insecurities.

Finally, try positive visualization. Imagine yourself in a positive light, and eventually, you will start to believe in the image you are picturing. Another way to use positive visualization is to imagine the person you want to be. Be very detailed and vivid in your imagination. Visualizing it will make it seem more like a possible reality than a lofty, vague picture. Doing this will motivate you to strive toward the goal and become who you want to be.

These are all how you can improve your self-love and body acceptance. The faster you learn to accept and love your body, the easier it will be to achieve self-love. However, constant barriers are still in your way, and you must remain vigilant against them. The next chapter helps you do this by warning you against the darker side of social media.

Chapter 6: Social Media and Its Delicious Poison

Most people use social media. It is hard to live without it, especially since it has some definite advantages, such as staying up to date with recent events, connecting with friends from around the globe, or even updating others about significant happenings in your life. Most people enjoy being on social media; it is a fun distraction. However, one major drawback to social media is its potential harm to your self-esteem and self-love. You must be aware of the impact of social media and how dangerous it is to rely on others' opinions for your validation. The more you care about what others think, the less value you will put on your opinion.

Social Media and Self-Love

Whether social media is a poison or a soothing balm to your self-love depends on how you interact with it. Though some people lose some self-love when they use social media, others gain more self-love. Social media is not an inherently harmful platform, and you stand to gain many benefits from it, provided you use it healthily. But what exactly are the healthy ways to use social media? What this boils down to are your intentions.

There are many healthy and happy reasons to be using social media. For example, you can use social media to connect with your friends, expand your professional network, join new communities to share your passions, stay in touch with family across the globe, share your life with others, or watch funny videos. All these reasons for using social media can improve your life and help you maintain your connections with others, which can benefit your mental health. Humans are not meant to be alone; they crave connections and meaningful bonds. When they have deep relationships with others, their self-esteem and self-love will naturally enhance. Social media can improve your self-love by helping you achieve and maintain your connections.

More specifically, your self-love can increase when you use social media if you use it to receive support. When you feel supported and provided for, you will feel safe and more easily believe in your worth. If others are helping you, you must be worthy of the help. Reaching out on social media and receiving social or practical support from your network can be a validating feeling. Knowing others care about you can encourage you to care about yourself, thereby increasing your self-love. For example, when you post on social media about something difficult you are struggling with, your network can respond to you, comfort you, encourage you, and offer their help. All of this will be a reminder that you are not alone and are part of a larger community looking out for one another. This sense of belonging and support will strengthen your self-love.

One thing to note is you should not post on social media with the sole intention of getting support because this will make your mental state heavily dependent on the type of response your post gets. If you do not get the response you want, your state of mind will spiral and darken. To prevent this reliance, you only need to tweak your mindset a little. Post your struggles to share with others, not to get sympathy and encouragement. This way, the act of posting itself will validate, and you will be fine if you do not get the response you want.

Other than linking you to others, social media can improve your self-love by connecting you to yourself, your emotions, and your experiences. A common trend on social media is to share almost everything about yourself—what you are thinking, feeling, doing, planning, changing or working toward. Posting online can act as an exercise in self-reflection, helping you stay in touch with yourself. Your self-awareness will improve, and thus your self-love will too.

All these benefits to your self-love will occur when you use social media in a healthy and balanced way. However, if you do not, then you stand to experience a lot of adverse effects. The most harmful thing social media can do to you amplifies your comparisons to others. On a good day, you may compare yourself to others and feel slightly worse about your life. When you mix in social media, it is like navigating a minefield of possible comparisons. Many people post on social media about how well their lives are going, what award they won, or what vacation they went on. Suppose you are in an excellent mental headspace. In that case, you can feel happy for your friends with only a twinge of good-natured envious—anyone would feel a little envy seeing their friend travel around the world, right? But if you choose to start comparing your lives, you will feel more dissatisfied with your own life, more self-conscious about your achievements, and simply bad about yourself. Interacting with social media in this way can steal your joy and replace your self-love with self-loathing.

Another way social media can harm your self-love is by increasing your daily stress. Have you ever posted something online and looked at it repeatedly throughout the day, checking for the number of likes, shares, or comments? These concerns will be racing through your head all day, increasing the stress you feel, and this is a sign you connect your self-worth and self-love to the responses you get from your posts. When you place too much emphasis on your posts, staking your self-love on them, you will naturally feel undue amounts of stress when you post. Your increased stress levels will decrease your self-care, indirectly hurting your self-love.

Moreover, you could see your posts as another area of comparison. Have you ever compared your post with someone else's, wondering why they have more likes or shares than you? Doing this can be a toxic way to use social media as you constantly make these comparisons and gradually feel worse about yourself until you lose significant amounts of self-love.

There is also the possibility of cyberbullying on social media, where you are exposed to many malicious comments and negative criticisms. Cyberbullying can destroy your self-esteem and amplify your self-doubt, thus decreasing your self-love. When you post things on social media, a wide variety of people may have access to it (depending on your privacy settings). While most of your connections online are genuine, sincere friends, there will always be a few random people who live to tear others down. Such people will say or comment terrible things to hurt you and damage your self-esteem. Though it is best to ignore such people, it can be easier said than done. It is easier to believe in the bad things people say than the good ones. And these random people online are all too eager to provide you with an excess of negative comments and malice. Once exposed to this negativity, it is a hard struggle not to be affected by it. Your self-love will undoubtedly take a hit.

As social media usage increases, levels of depression and anxiety also rise in teens and kids. It could be a sign that more people are using social media in unhealthy ways and harming their self-love rather than using it in healthy ways to increase their self-love. Rather than feeling connected with others, supported, and in touch with themselves, they are experiencing more comparisons, stress, and negative feedback online. There have been studies on the link between social media and mental health, and one specific study revealed teenagers who spent more than three hours every day on social media were more likely to develop mental health problems (Auld, 2019). The possible mental health problems you can develop due to social media include anxiety, depression, loneliness, or negative self-image. Constantly worrying about how others may respond to your post or that your post is not getting enough likes could lead to anxiety. When you are constantly comparing yourself to others and feeling worse about yourself and your life, this could lead to depression.

Loneliness will develop when you compare yourself to others and decide you are inferior, thus preferring to isolate yourself. Or else loneliness can come when you see everyone's posts where they spend time with each other, and you begin to feel left out. It is easy to guess how a negative self-image can be created through social media. When you look at others' posts and see their bodies or their achievements, you will put yourself down in comparison, thus creating a negative body image and self-image. Social media can overload you with pictures of others leading seemingly perfect lives or having seemingly ideal bodies, creating unrealistic expectations for what you consider normal and desirable. Forcing yourself to live by and strive toward these unrealistic expectations can continually harm your self-esteem and self-love.

Knowing how social media can make or break your self-love will help you become more aware of how you use it. Do you want to use social media in ways to help you or harm you? The power is all in your hands. It is best to make conscious choices about how you engage with social media to control how it impacts your self-love. When you do this, you will be able to recognize when social media is negatively affecting your self-love and take steps to address it. If the impact of social media is too severe for you to handle on your own, you should seek professional help. Remember, self-love is a journey, and it is crucial to be patient with yourself and to practice self-compassion throughout the process. At the same time, it is important to remember social media is one aspect of your life. It can be a great source of validation and self-worth (when you use it to form connections with others), but it should not be the only source. If you find yourself relying too much on social media for validation, try branching out and exploring different sources of self-worth, such as personal relationships, hobbies, competitions, and accomplishments.

Caring Too Much About What Others Think

Knowing the positive and negative ways of interacting with social media is excellent, but what if you still need to tell which camp you fall into? An easy way to know if you are using social media negatively is if you care too much about what others think. When you use social media in a harmful way, you will become overly reliant on likes, comments, and positive responses from others. In other words, the opinions of others will have a lot of power over you. If others like you, then you like yourself too. If others dislike you, then you tear yourself apart, trying to fix the parts of yourself you imagine they do not like. Living like this can significantly hinder developing self-love because you will naturally become more self-critical and self-conscious. You will always be worried about how others see you and place yourself under a microscope trying to find potential flaws or mistakes. You will also bend over backward, trying to please others or changing yourself to suit the opinions of others. Doing this will decrease your self-worth as you let others walk all over you, thus negatively affecting your self-love as well.

There are many reasons why you care too much about what others think. For one, you may fear rejection or disapproval. In your mind, rejection may be a comment on your worth. To avoid feeling worthless, you do all you can to avoid rejection, even if this means changing yourself. Another reason could be you lack self-confidence and self-esteem, and thus you try to gain these things through the approval of others. If you can get others to like you more, you will also like yourself. Whatever your reason for caring too much about what others think, you must notice this behavior to ensure you can take positive steps to change and improve. Here are some signs you will exhibit if you have this habit:

You change yourself when others criticize something about you, no matter who criticizes you or whether you trust them.

- You are indecisive and need help to make decisions for yourself.
- You do not set your boundaries; even when you do, you do not enforce them.
- You are a perfectionist, wanting to be seen as perfect by others.
- You do not voice your opinion if it differs from others or if you think others will not agree or approve.
- Your mental state will sharply deteriorate if you believe someone dislikes or disapproves of you.
- You find it hard to say no.
- You constantly apologize, whether or not you did anything wrong.

If you can relate to these signs, then you are someone who places too much emphasis on the opinions of others and needs more focus on your own. This trait can make social media more harmful to your self-love. However, fear not! There are many exercises you will receive to help you overcome these struggles.

Exercises to Treat Social Media's Poison

Once you have noticed social media's damaging effects on you, you can begin the treatment process. Do not worry; all these exercises are simple. You need to tweak your mindset slightly to transform social media from poisonous to affirming.

You must first expect and accept that other people will have their thoughts, beliefs, and opinions about you. Judgments and assessments are natural elements of social interaction. You do it yourself during your everyday interactions. You cannot expect to be exempt from something ingrained in every interaction. Being assessed is unavoidable; all you can do is learn to expect it. When you wish for judgments and assessments, you will stop feeling worried and apprehensive. You will be more able to live in the moment.

After learning to expect it, you must also learn to accept the opinions of others. You cannot control the thoughts of others. Do not destroy yourself trying to do the impossible. Instead, accept it; this will help you let go and be less affected by their opinions. One important note is that because you accept others have an opinion about you, it does not mean you accept their views as accurate or factual. Remind yourself how others will have their beliefs, which may often be wrong, which will help you be less affected by their views.

Another way to be less affected by the opinions of others is to practice mindfulness. When others express negative views of you, it is easy to feel bad about yourself and drown in your negative emotions. Mindfulness can help snap you out of it by reducing your anxiety. When you start to feel insecure and anxious, you can get stuck on a particular thought or emotion and obsess over it, allowing it to overwhelm your mind and take over your thoughts. Mindfulness prevents this from happening by helping you stay present at the moment. You will be more aware and accepting of your emotions and ideas. This self-acceptance can help you cope better with your negativity. To practice mindfulness, follow these steps:

1. Sit upright in a comfortable position.
2. Breathe in for four seconds, then breathe out for four seconds.

3. As you focus on your breathing, observe your thoughts and emotions. Accept these are your thoughts and feelings, look at them, and let them go. Do not hold onto any of them; let them ebb and flow. Try not to be affected by what you are observing.

You may care too much about what others think because you do not have a robust and stable sense of self. If you do not know who you are, you are more likely to let others decide for you. You will rely on others to tell you who you are or what you should do. To prevent this, you have to take the time to reflect on yourself and build your own identity.

Remember, this is your life, and you must choose the kind of person you want to be. Here are some starter questions you can use to explore your identity:

- How would you describe yourself?
- What are things important to you?
- What are you passionate about?
- What makes you worried, excited, happy, sad, or angry?
- What are your goals in life?
- How do you want others to see you?
- How do you want others to remember you?
- What effect do you want to have on others or the world?

You can even ask yourself more specific questions to clarify your values in life. When you know what matters to you and abide by those values, you will care less about the criticisms of others because you will be confident in the knowledge you are living by your values. In this way, clarifying your values can increase your self-confidence and self-love. To explore what your values may be, ask yourself:

- What frustrates you in life? Why do you think this frustrates you?
- What items are on your bucket list? What do these items say about you? What are they prioritizing?

- Is there anything you passionately believe in, even if others do not agree with you?
- What qualities are important to you?
- What habits are essential to you?

The following exercise is simple—you do not have to do anything. It is asking you *not* to do something. For this exercise, all you have to do is not assume what others are thinking. When using social media, you often assume the worst in the opinions of others. You will worry excessively about what others think of you and conjure up the worst possible thoughts others may have of you, which can be stressful and unproductive since you cannot possibly know what others are thinking. To avoid feeling unwarranted stress and anxiety, you must stop assuming what others think of you.

All the exercises above can help you care less about what others think and interact with social media in healthier ways. Let's move to exercises you can use if you have decided to reduce your social media usage.

Sometimes the best way to use social media is to use it less. This way, it has less chance to harm your self-love, and you can begin to regain a healthy balance in your life. The first exercise to achieve this is keeping your phone away from your bed and dining table. Most screen time occurs when you are in bed, relaxing, or during mealtimes. If you keep your phone away from you at these times, you can significantly reduce your social media usage. It may be hard to keep your phone away from you at night because you use it for your alarm. In this case, put your phone on silent mode and set it aside. Then it is a question of your willpower not to use your phone anymore. But at least you will not have any notifications to tempt you. It is easier not to use the phone at the dining table. Put it in another room or in your bag. Focus instead on the meal in front of you. Try to savor the dish, live in the present moment, and enjoy the people you are eating with. Rather than looking at your screen, try connecting with the people right before you.

Other than your phone's location, you can reduce your social media usage by turning off your notifications. Every social media app has the option to customize your notifications. Take advantage of this to switch off all your notifications; this may lessen your anxiety and stress as you will no longer wait to see how many people liked or commented on your post. Over time, you will become less reliant on the responses and opinions of others.

You can also schedule your posts. Suppose you have been very active on social media until now. In that case, it can be hard for you to reduce your activity suddenly. A schedule will give you something to look forward to daily while limiting your interaction with social media. Allow yourself one post per day at a specific time, and it will become a habit. Try to keep yourself from posting more often. Remember, the whole point is slowly reducing your reliance on social media. It is best to be disciplined and dedicated to making this change.

If you are addicted to social media, reducing your screen time will be all the more challenging. You may find yourself obsessing over possible posts, wondering about what others are posting, or constantly reaching for your phone. If you are getting restless, it is important to stay busy. People often go on social media when they have nothing better to do. It is possible to waste hours upon hours scrolling through videos and posts. Do not allow yourself to be tempted by this. Instead, keep busy to ensure you do not even think about social media. Pick up a new hobby, join a dance class, start gardening, or buy a new book to read. There are endless amounts of activities you could fill your day with.

Easing off social media and placing less emphasis on the opinions of others are not changes you can achieve overnight. It will be a slow process; be patient, and give yourself time to adjust. Slowly but surely, you will see improvements and begin to feel more self-love. The next chapter guides you to love your failures and successes, further supercharging your self-love.

Chapter 7: Loving Your Failings and Achievements

In life, you will inevitably have your ups and downs, pride and shame, losses and success. It is best to acknowledge how all these aspects make up your life. Do not try to reject any part of your experiences. You cannot cherry-pick those aspects of your existence you want and those you wish to discard. They are all threads interweaved to create the beautiful tapestry of your lived experience. Do not invalidate your experiences by trying to reject one part of them. Instead, show yourself love by accepting your failings and achievements, as they are both essential aspects that makeup who you are. Once you do this, your self-worth and self-love will both benefit you.

Self-Worth and Self-Love

Self-worth interacts with self-love in significant ways. It is easier to have one with the other. But what exactly is self-worth anyways? Self-worth is how much you value yourself and your confidence in your abilities. There are many factors influencing how much self-worth you have:

Personal values and beliefs: If you know your values and try to live by them, you will feel a greater sense of purpose and fulfillment, increasing your self-worth. If you do not know your values, you will feel more lost in life and unsure of your decisions, which can decrease your self-worth.

Accomplishments and achievements: When you perform well in something and even get the tangible proof you excel (such as a medal, a certificate, or a top grade), you will become more confident in your abilities, thus increasing your self-worth. Recognizing and celebrating your accomplishments can do wonders for your self-worth.

Positive relationships: When you have deep and meaningful relationships, you will be connected to a network of people who love and support you. These connections can assure you of your worth, as they will all believe you are capable and worthy of love. When people you trust think this of you, it will be easier for you to accept and internalize those messages.

Self-care and self-compassion: The more you cultivate these traits, the higher your self-worth will be. When you take care of yourself and treat yourself with kindness and compassion, you indirectly tell yourself you are someone who deserves to be treated this way, thus increasing your self-worth.

Inner qualities: When you value certain traits in yourself, you can work to increase or strengthen those traits, further improving your self-worth. For example, suppose you value kindness, compassion, intelligence, or integrity. In that case, you can notice these traits in yourself and love yourself more because of it, increasing your self-worth.

External factors like appearance, material possession, or societal status can influence self-worth. Still, it is best to minimize the effects of these factors. When your self-worth relies on external factors, it can be more volatile and hard to maintain. Instead, focus more on your values, beliefs, and inner qualities. You can even emphasize your strengths by recognizing and celebrating your accomplishments, whether big or small.

Acknowledging these can validate and identify your strengths and successes. However, be careful not to stake your entire self-worth on only your achievements. Doing this can be dangerous as it suggests you will no longer be worthy once you stop achieving, which is an unhealthy assumption. To circumvent this belief, you must base your self-worth on all the factors listed above in a balanced way. Remember to emphasize the importance of one factor over another. Your self-worth should be determined by various things, not only your accomplishments. Also, one thing self-worth should never be determined by is the opinions of others. How much you value yourself should have nothing to do with how others cherish you. It is your relationship with yourself; focus on yourself and not on others.

Since self-worth measures how much you value and believe in yourself, it is simple to see how more self-worth can result in more self-love. When you respect yourself more, you will treat yourself more lovingly. When you believe in yourself more, you will feel more confident. Therefore, increasing your self-worth is a viable way to get to self-love. But before working on your self-worth, you must work out your relationship between success and failure.

Why Failing Is Important

You have been cautioned not to overemphasize your accomplishments when trying to increase your self-worth. However, this can be a hard habit to break. An overemphasis on achievements may be ingrained in you at this point. If this is the case, you must slowly undo all the mindsets you have created from this bad habit. One common negative mindset is an aversion to failure. In your mind, since accomplishments add to your worth, failures would detract from them. With this type of thinking, it is clear why you would develop an aversion and fear toward collapse. If every loss takes something away from your value as a person, you will do everything in your power to avoid failing. And when you inevitably fail—no one can avoid failure forever—this mindset amplifies your negative reaction, causing you undue stress and anguish.

To change this mindset and lessen your aversion to failure, you must realize failing is a necessary experience in life. Success would be preferable, but it is not the end of the world when you fail. Failure can mark the very beginning of your progress. There are many ways you can benefit from failure. Firstly, you gain experience from it. When you fail, it means you tried something, and it did not work, and this can give you a lot of valuable information you can use the next time. You could adjust certain aspects of your technique or choose a different approach altogether. Whatever you decide, your experience with failure will be right there with you, informing your decisions. The firsthand experience you gain through your losses will help you understand yourself, the task, your approach, and your struggles more in-depth. The experience and knowledge you gain from failures are invaluable. Every time you fail, you gain new information you can use to increase your chances of success the next time.

The second benefit you stand to gain from failing is resilience. For some people, the moment they fail is the moment they decide to throw in the towel. They are done after one attempt. Do not let this be you. Keep trying, keep working, and keep failing. The more you fail, the greater the resilience you build for yourself. You will be able to keep trying no matter what, developing an iron will, and you will not quit until you have finally tasted success. The more you fail, the more challenging your mindset becomes and your chances of sticking with it until you succeed. People without resilience will expect to succeed on the first try and get very crushed when they do not. But once you develop your strength, you will be okay even if you do not succeed the first ten times. You will pick yourself back up and keep trying. When you have resilience, it does not matter how often you fail—you will keep working, and eventually, you will succeed.

Failure is vital because it helps you grow. Someone who has never tasted the bitterness of defeat or faced challenges in their life will never be able to grow. Only after you struggle and fail can you grow and develop yourself. After failing a few times, you will learn what true motivation feels like and may even discover a deeper understanding of your life and how your mind works. Or else you will learn to zoom out and focus on the big picture to gain new perspectives rather than getting bogged down by the little details of your failure. There are countless ways in which failure can help you grow as a person. Rather than feeling afraid or apprehensive about failure, lean into it when it happens. Ask yourself what you can learn from this experience.

How to Learn From Failure

If you are having difficulty changing your failures into lessons, here are some tips you can use. The first step is to reflect on your experience. What went wrong? What could you have done differently? How could you have changed the outcome? What can you do better next time? What did you do well this time? What went right? These questions can help you pinpoint what areas you can improve on and what things you did well. Doing this will increase your self-awareness and allow you to capitalize on your strengths and minimize your weaknesses the next time.

Another line of thought you can try is identifying the cause of your failure. Did you fail because you used the wrong technique? Was it performance anxiety? Were you unprepared? Did you need to gain a particular skill or knowledge? Once you understand why you failed this time, you can take action to avoid those causes in the future. This type of reflection prevents you from making the same mistakes again. As you are reflecting, you must be honest with yourself. Do not try to push the blame elsewhere. Openly seek the actual cause of your failure without judgment. By reducing the judgment and criticism you have, you encourage yourself to be more honest with yourself about your role in what happened, and this will allow you to take full responsibility for your actions without blaming others or making excuses for yourself.

If self-reflection is hard for you, this is okay. You can still learn from your failures by seeking feedback from others who were there and who observed your performance. Ask for feedback from people you trust, people involved in the situation, or people with experience and knowledge in the relevant fields. These people will be able to give you reliable and helpful feedback on how you can improve. They may even offer different perspectives on the situation.

Once you get feedback from others or reflect on yourself, you must try to plan how to address the areas needing fixing. It is not enough to know what went wrong; you should also try to make things go right. For this step, remember to be patient with yourself. You may find the solution later, but trust you have the resources and abilities to find the best way forward. And do not be afraid to ask others for advice.

After you plan, put it into action and see how things go. Once you have implemented the changes, see how they affect the result. If you succeed, awesome! It means your analysis of yourself was accurate, and your changes were effective. If you fail again, no worries; try again. Repeat the process of self-reflection and planning, then put this new plan into action. Keep repeating this process until you succeed.

This process can be a long and hard one. Therefore, you must stay positive throughout. It is only a definite failure when you choose to give up. As long as you keep trying, success continues to be a possibility. Keep your chin up and continue trying. Even if you do not immediately achieve success, you can at least rest easy in the knowledge you are constantly learning and growing from the process. By keeping a positive mindset, you help keep yourself motivated and prevent yourself from giving up. Another perspective you could benefit from is learning to let go of your failures. Suppose you obsess over every single failure you have ever experienced. In that case, you may focus more on your adverse reactions to those failures than on how you can benefit and learn from those experiences. Rather than obsessing over your failures, try to let go of them to reduce their power over you. Once you do, you can more easily learn from them. Failure is not final. You can always learn and grow from them and try again another day. With a positive attitude, the right mindset, and a plan of action, you can turn your failings into valuable learning experiences.

How to Acknowledge and Appreciate Achievements

With the tips above, you can improve your relationship with your failures. You will no longer be afraid or apprehensive toward them; instead, you will be able to learn and grow from them. But what about your relationship with your achievements? There are a few kinds of negative relationships you may have with your achievements. One of the more damaging ones is when you refuse to acknowledge and appreciate your successes, which can occur for several reasons. You may live a busy lifestyle and not have the time or energy to notice your achievements. You might have low self-esteem and thus feel uncomfortable praising yourself. Or you are a perfectionist who criticizes your achievements for not being perfect. You do not acknowledge and appreciate your achievements for many reasons. However, if this continues, it will be hard to raise your self-worth as you will never come to value or believe in yourself more. To increase your self-worth, you need to learn how to acknowledge your achievements. The following goes over how you can do this!

For one, you can reflect on your life and scan it for your successes and high points. In what moments are you most proud of yourself? What instances show your good decision-making skills? What struggles have you battled and conquered? Write down everything that comes to mind, whether big or small. If you need to remember many successes, list your daily accomplishments. What are you proud of doing every day? At the end of every day, try to list three things you accomplished today. These do not need to be significant, lofty, or challenging achievements. List down whatever you did today and feel good about it. For example, you may have gotten a lot of errands finished, or perhaps you comforted a loved one when they opened up to you.

Other than reflecting on yourself, try complimenting yourself while looking in the mirror. Tell yourself what you are doing well, or remind yourself of what you have done well. By repeating kind, loving, affirming messages to yourself about your current and past achievements, you will eventually internalize those messages and start to believe them. You will learn more about affirmations in the next chapter so stick around!

If you like to write, you can even make a blog about your achievements. This blog can be private or public, whichever makes you more comfortable. The main point is to write about your past accomplishments to ensure you have written descriptions about how you struggled, persevered, and triumphed. As you write about your past success, you may discover you are more striking and impressive than you thought. Plus, if your blog is public, you may inspire others with your stories, connecting with and influencing others positively and affirmatively.

Exercises to Increase Self-Worth

Failures and successes are essential parts of your experiences. You should embrace, accept, and love them rather than accept and reject the other. This being said, you should not use either of these experiences to influence your self-worth. If your self-worth relies on external factors, it will not be stable or balanced. Your self-worth must come from within, from a constant and steady belief that you are worthy of love, care, and respect. To achieve a strong self-worth like this:

1. List all the things you love about yourself.
2. Include your traits, personality, strengths, and quirks, but do not include your achievements.
3. Suppose you continue to link your self-worth and self-love to your accomplishments.

Move your focus away from your achievements and open your heart to other lovable facts about yourself. In that case, they will continue to be unsteady and unreliable. Take some time to reflect on yourself and find things you genuinely love about yourself. Are you kind, sensitive, empathetic, funny, or a good listener? Do you love how you are assertive, soft-spoken, a bookworm, a natural leader, or a good follower?

The following exercise asks you to redefine your idea of success. When you think of success, what images come to mind? These are your automatic assumptions about success. Now, take some time to think about what would really make you happy in life and what success would look like for you specifically. Refrain from deferring to the ideal image of success you see on television or social media. There is more than one version of success suitable for everyone. You may have your own understanding, which is unique to you. Success is filling your days doing what you love, focusing on meaningful relationships, or working at a job you believe positively affects the world. Society commonly measures success by money and awards, but you do not have to abide by this. Redefine what success means to direct your life where you want it to go rather than chasing something society says you should. When pursuing what you want, you will feel better about yourself as you live life by your standards, increasing your self-worth and self-love. Plus, you will be more motivated and thus more likely to achieve your goals and further improve your self-worth.

Another way to strengthen your self-worth is to reflect on yourself and find the parts of you which remain constant throughout. No matter where you are, who you are with, what you are doing, or how well you have performed, this part of you never changes. You could have scored the highest on an exam or gotten dead last in a competition, and either way, this part of you is unaffected. Once you find this part of yourself, you will better understand who you are. Then, you can tell yourself no matter how many achievements or failures you encounter in the future. They will not change who you are at your core. Telling yourself this can validate and affirm your sense of self, thus increasing your self-worth.

Finally, to increase your self-worth, try to practice unconditional self-care. Do not dole out your self-care practices when you think you finally deserve them. Do it unconditionally to inform yourself how you deserve love and care, no matter what. You do not have to do or achieve anything to be worthy of love; you must exist and be yourself. Practice self-care often to reinforce to yourself how you are worthy of love. Some ways to practice self-care are to forgive yourself when you make mistakes, treat yourself to a nice bath, or take more breaks from work. When you remind yourself you are worthy of love, your self-worth and self-love will grow more robust.

Affirmations are the last helpful habit, in this book, you can incorporate to increase your self-love. In the next chapter, you will discover how affirmations can help you and how you can practice them.

Chapter 8: Affirmations

The previous chapter briefly touched on affirmations and how they can help you acknowledge yourself and increase your self-worth. Now, let's go into depth on how affirmations work and how you can benefit from them. An affirmation is a saying, statement, or phrase you repeat to yourself, intending to uplift, encourage, and comfort you, brightening your perspective and increasing your self-love. Affirmations can be a powerful weapon against self-destructive, self-critical, and self-limiting thoughts. For example, when you think you are worthless or incapable of dealing with your current struggles, affirmations can encourage and convince you of ways you are more capable than you think. Affirmations combat the negativity that sometimes steals into your life and helps replace those negative thoughts with positive ones. When you repeat affirmations to yourself, you actively choose positivity over negativity. You are acknowledging your harmful thoughts and consciously trying to overcome them, decisive actions and choice in your life.

There are even unconscious effects of repeating affirmations. Even if you do not fully believe in what you are repeating to yourself at first, eventually, you will learn to internalize those messages. Your subconscious mind will slowly begin to accept the meanings you keep repeating to yourself, gradually changing its orientation to be more loving and favorable to you. In this way, affirmations can improve your self-love.

No matter what kind of issue you are dealing with, whether it is weight loss, career advancement, self-esteem, stress, motivation, self-confidence, or relationship problems, you can create an affirmation to offer support and encouragement. Affirmations can also be used to focus on specific goals or areas of improvement. But this is not all affirmations can do. You can tailor your affirmations to target specific beliefs and aims to motivate yourself in those areas. You would be surprised to know how diverse affirmations can be. To help you understand, let's look at a few examples of affirmations addressing various aspects of your life:

- I am worthy and deserving of love and happiness. (This affirmation can address your self-love issues).
- It is okay to fail as long as I learn from my mistakes. (This affirmation can address your issues with failure).
- I have the ability to improve my relationships. I deserve to be treated well by others. (This affirmation can address your relationship issues).
- If I work hard, I can achieve my goals. (This affirmation can address your motivation issues).

As you can see, affirmations can be tailored to suit a wide variety of your needs. Do not hesitate to start using them and benefitting from them! Before you do, though, you must figure out the best way to use affirmations. They can be written down, spoken, or even visualized. It is essential to choose the method that is most impactful for you. Then, it is time to determine what affirmation you want to repeat to yourself. Choose one specific to your needs and one that resonates deeply with you. And remember, affirmations alone are not enough to change your life. They are additional tools you can use to help yourself on your journey, but at the end of the day, it is all up to you, your actions, and your consistent effort. Ensure you try hard to reach your goals instead of relying solely on affirmations. At the same time, remember to be patient with yourself. You may not see results right away, but give it time. Soon you will see the fruits of all your labor!

How to Create and Use Affirmations

Before reaping the benefits of your affirmations, you must create one for yourself. Making an affirmation for yourself can ensure it is specific to your needs and it resonates with you. The first step is to think about the area you want to improve. What is the focus of your affirmation going to be? Do you want to focus on increasing your self-love, enhancing your relationship with your family, overcoming your procrastination, or developing a new healthy habit? Write down the goals you want to achieve with the help of your affirmations. It does not have to be only one, either. You can create several affirmations, all specific to the various goals you are aiming for. Make sure you know what you want and why you want it. Making an affirmation pointed at a goal and not aligned with your values and priorities, will not be effective. This is because your heart will not be in it in the first place. Affirmations work best when you are fired up to work toward the goal.

The second step is to ensure your affirmation is realistic, honest, and achievable. If the affirmation you create is unattainable or out of your control, such as "I will grow two inches," you are setting yourself up for failure, frustration, and disappointment. The same goes for if you create an affirmation not based on a realistic assessment of your skills, such as saying, "I will win this upcoming swimming competition," when you are still learning how to swim. Your affirmations need to be realistically based on your abilities. This way, you push yourself to your limits to achieve the most you can. Suppose you set unrealistic and unattainable affirmations for yourself. In that case, you will only feel worse about yourself for not living up to them. You will begin to feel discouraged, despairing, and downcasted. Save yourself this undue anguish and keep your affirmations realistic!

The enemy of positive affirmations is negative self-talk. Many times, when you start using positive affirmations more, your negative self-talk may amplify. In these cases, you must transform all the negativity into positivity. What is a common negative thought or theme which is hurting you? What affirmation can you create to combat and replace this negativity with positivity? Often, you can create practical and positive affirmations simply by saying the opposite of what your negative self-talk is saying to you. For example, if your inner critic says, "You are worthless," you can counter it by telling yourself, "I am worthy of love and care." If your inner critic says, "You are a failure in your career," you can create a positive affirmation by saying, "I have the skills and knowledge needed to excel in my job."

Once you have written down your affirmations, read through them and ensure they are all written in the present tense. This little switch in tenses can make a difference in how your mind processes your affirmations. Suppose you write it in the past tense. In that case, your mind will distance yourself from your affirmations, thinking they are relevant to the past and not the present and would minimize the benefits you gain from them. For example, if you write, "I excelled in my job," the past tense makes it easier for your inner critic to increase your self-doubt and question whether you are excelling in your job currently. Suppose you write it in the future tense. In that case, your mind will procrastinate on any changes you want to make in the present, putting it off as your future responsibility. It can delay the positive changes you could be making. For example, if you write, "I will excel in my job," you may imagine a vague future construct where you excel. This vague idea makes it harder for you to initiate any positive action in the present.

In contrast, when you write your affirmations in the present tense, it sounds like it is already happening. What you say is relevant to you right now, and you must make the changes you want in the present. For example, when you write, "I excel in my job," it is easier to believe it could be true. You will feel more motivated to take the necessary actions to make it true.

As you check the tenses in your affirmations, you can look out for another aspect of language: positive or negative words. Affirmations should be affirming. To this end, avoid words like "cannot" or "not." Instead, use words like "can" and "will." For example, instead of saying, "I will not slack off on my fitness," try saying, "I will emphasize my fitness." The former affirmation asks you not to do something, which may make you more passive about your goal. The latter affirmation charges you to do something to make changes actively. It can increase your passion and dedication to your objective.

Another tip to increase the effectiveness of your affirmations is to repeat them with emotional weight behind them. Only repeat them with feeling. Imbue each affirmation with knowledge of your end goal and passion for seeing them through. Before you repeat each affirmation to yourself, remember why they are important and meaningful to you. Why are you taking the trouble to repeat these affirmations to yourself? What is at stake here? When you remind yourself of your greater purpose, you will be more passionate about repeating your affirmations, and the affirmations, in turn, will be more powerful and effective.

Other than repeating your affirmations with feelings, it is best to repeat them regularly. You may not remember if you only repeat your affirmations once a week. Thus they will have minimal benefits for you. But suppose you repeat your affirmations to yourself every day. In that case, you will slowly but surely change your thinking pattern to be more positive, affirming, and optimistic.

You can try to repeat your affirmations to yourself when you wake up, allowing you to start your day on a positive note. When you repeat your affirmations to yourself, try to repeat each one about 10 times, giving yourself enough time and space to absorb the message and meaning of each affirmation. Give yourself about 5 to 10 minutes to finish repeating all your affirmations. Take your time, repeat them slowly, listen to yourself, and focus on the words as you are saying them. Try to believe in what you are saying. And it does not have to be you repeating your affirmations, either. You can ask a trusted friend or family member to repeat your affirmations. It may be easier to believe in them when you hear them from someone else.

You can use affirmations in three main ways: saying them out loud, writing them down, and visualizing them. You do not need to pick only one; you can combine them all and see which works best for you. The first method is speaking your affirmations out loud. Do not merely think of them to yourself. Speak them out loud because this can reinforce their message in your mind, making them more effective. The second method is writing them down and placing them somewhere you will see them often. Seeing them will serve as a constant reminder of your affirmations. You can combine this with the first method by reading the affirmations out loud every time you see them.

The third method is visualization, in which you close your eyes and vividly imagine yourself achieving your affirmation. Having a clear picture of your end goal can strongly motivate you.

Whichever method you choose, you must combine your affirmations with action. Affirmations can convince you that you can achieve your goals, but they cannot acquire them. Those actions and changes need to come from you. Put in the effort to live up to your affirmations. Remember to be patient and consistent. Stay calm if you do not see results as quickly as you would like. Keep trying consistently, and you will eventually reach your destination. Remember, this is a journey.

Benefits of Affirmations

Affirmations are a valuable tool to help you replace negative thoughts and beliefs with positive ones and implement positive change in your life. However, a tool can only help you if you pick it up and put in the effort for yourself. You will not see much change if you use affirmations but do not put in the work. Conversely, if you use affirmations in tandem with sincere effort, there is no limit to how much you can improve your life! Though affirmations can make the job smoother, you still have to do the work, meaning the extent of benefits you gain from affirmations depends on you.

One benefit you stand to gain from affirmations is improving your self-esteem and self-confidence. When you are overwhelmed by negative thoughts and beliefs, your self-esteem and self-confidence will be at rock bottom. You will be steeped in self-critical and harsh judgments about yourself, increasing your self-doubt and self-loathing. However, once you switch those thoughts out for positive ones, you will be comforted by more understanding, kind, and compassionate thoughts toward yourself.

You will even enjoy increased motivation and creativity. Your affirmations are typically focused and directed toward specific goals to hone your attention and keep you focused on achieving a particular purpose. Your positive thinking will also enable you to stay motivated and not give up, even when things get hard or you encounter failure. As for your creativity, affirmations can inspire your creativity by encouraging you to think outside the box and try new approaches. Linking to your motivation, as well, the longer you keep at something, the more various techniques you can try. Give yourself enough space and time to try new things, experiment, and explore!

Finally, affirmations can help reduce your stress and anxiety. The very act of repeating affirmations to yourself tells you how you are taking positive actions in your life to enact specific changes. You are taking control of your life and deciding what to do for yourself, which can be empowering, thus increasing your self-confidence. When you are more sure of yourself, your abilities, and your decisions, your stress and anxiety will naturally decrease.

Affirmations for Self-Love

Though you already have a guide on creating your affirmations, you could still benefit from some examples and templates for self-love affirmations. Here are some possible self-love affirmations you could use to model your own. These affirmations are more specifically geared to help your self-worth and self-acceptance (Taylor, 2020):

- I accept myself exactly as I am now.
- No matter what, I accept myself.
- I extend love to myself and accept love.
- I am okay with where I am now.
- I love who I am.
- I am perfect, exactly like this; I do not need to change anything.
- I give myself love, and it is enough.
- I am enough.
- I am whole.
- I am always growing and learning from my experiences.

These affirmations are more for your self-esteem and self-forgiveness:

- I forgive myself.

- What happened is in the past and I make my peace with it.
- I am proud of who I am becoming.
- I am beautiful in every way.
- I am trying my best, and it is enough.
- I am learning to forgive myself.
- Loving myself is a process I am getting better at.
- I am a work in progress.
- I am learning to see myself in new ways.
- I let go of all the thoughts and beliefs which are hurting me.
- I deserve love.

There are even affirmations to help your confidence:

- I am a fantastic person.
- I love my body and my personality.
- Self-love is a priority for me.
- I deserve love and respect.
- My imperfections make me unique.
- Being myself is enough; I do not need to be anyone else.
- My physical body does not define me.
- I choose to love myself, not despite my flaws but because of them.
- I am capable and strong.
- I choose myself.
- I have the ability to get through this.

Finally, there are affirmations to increase your self-love in general:

- I love myself.
- I am loved.
- I choose to accept love.
- Others love me, and I do too.
- I love myself unconditionally.
- No matter what failures or successes I encounter in life, I love myself.

- Love is everywhere; it is all around me.
- I accept love from myself and others.
- I love myself deeply and fully.
- Love is always available to me if I choose it.

If you need inspiration for your affirmations, look through the examples here. You can model your own after these and tailor them to suit your goals and needs. After you do, you can start using affirmations in your daily life!

Please Leave A Review

Hey there!

Have you ever read a book that changed your life? A book that gave you practical strategies to improve your self-love and increase your confidence? If you've read Truly, Madly, Deeply Love YOU: How to love yourself by improving self-esteem and self-confidence, you know the value it brings.

Now, imagine if you could help someone else find that same value. By leaving a review, you can help others experience the transformation this book can provide. So, are you ready to make a difference in someone's life?

By leaving a review for Truly, Madly, Deeply Love YOU, you can deliver value to others during their reading experience. Your words can help someone decide if this book is right for them, ultimately leading them to a happier, more fulfilling life.

But why do we need reviews? Well, in today's world, reviews are crucial for getting the word out about a product or service. They help people make informed decisions and trust the recommendations of others. When someone is searching for a self-help book like Truly, Madly, Deeply Love YOU, your review could be the deciding factor in buying the book.

So, here's the ask: if you've read Truly, Madly, Deeply Love YOU, please leave an honest review. Whether you loved it or didn't find it helpful, your feedback is valuable. It can help other readers make a decision and ultimately help them improve their own lives.

Leaving a review is easy. Simply go to the Amazon page for the book, scroll down to the "Customer Reviews" section, and click "Write a customer review." Then, share your thoughts and feelings about the book.

The impact of leaving a review goes beyond just helping other readers. It also helps the author and encourages them to continue creating valuable content. And as a reader, you can feel good knowing that you helped someone else find a book that could potentially change their life.

Let's spread the love and positivity that Truly, Madly, Deeply Love YOU promotes. Leave a review today and help someone else find the value in this life-changing book.

Thank you for considering leaving a review for Truly, Madly, Deeply Love YOU. Your words could make all the difference in someone's life.

Now let's continue to the final chapter.

Conclusion

Loving Yourself

The decision to love yourself is essential. Luckily, with the skills, tips, and tools you have received from this book, you are well-equipped and well-prepared to deal with whatever obstacles you face. Once you have made it, you embark on a long journey of self-discovery and self-healing.

With the knowledge of the 10 selves of self-love from Chapter 1, you have a deeper understanding of self-love. You can pinpoint what aspect of your self-love needs work. If you struggle with self-loathing, the information from Chapter 2 can help you approach your situation with more compassion and kindness. You even received exercises to overcome your self-loathing. If you value relationships, Chapter 3 guided you through how self-love can improve your friendships and romantic relationships. You then discovered how to walk away from toxic relationships and build more positive connections with others. Acknowledging how depression is a rampant concern, Chapter 4 explored how you can more readily accept positivity from others and what exercises you can use to alleviate your symptoms of depression. Even if you have a mental illness, self-love is always available!

Chapter 5 dealt with the issue of poor self-images and body images. You examined where insecurities come from and what exercises you can use to increase your self-love and body acceptance. Body image issues are often caused by social media, which Chapter 6 warned you about. Social media is not unhealthy, but once you start to care too much about what others think, it can harm your self-love. To avoid this outcome, you were led through exercises to stop overemphasizing the opinions of others and to reduce your social media usage. Chapter 7 moved on to address your self-worth, how to learn from failures, how to acknowledge success, and what exercises can increase your self-worth. Finally, Chapter 8 explained how you could create and use affirmations to your benefit. All this information is now at your fingertips, ready to help you out whenever called upon.

The most important thing to remember throughout all this is to keep trying. You will not get it all right, and you will not get it right all the time, but as long as you keep trying, there is no way for you to fail! Of course, there will be times when things get hard, and you feel like giving up. In those instances, take a mental health day, do some self-care activities, and do whatever you think will encourage you to keep trying.

It is okay to take a day off from working on self-love. Having a day off from self-love exercises and treating yourself to something nice will help keep you motivated and energized to stay on your self-love journey. With days off, you can stay on course in the long run and eventually cultivate a healthy amount of self-love. Also, being aware of how you are feeling and taking measures to take care of yourself is a form of self-love. It sounds paradoxical, but sometimes taking a break from your self-love exercises and practices can be a form of self-love! With all the effort you have been putting in, you deserve a break! Try to figure out what specific self-care or self-love acts you can do to keep yourself happy and motivated. Give yourself a break from your self-love exercises for the day, and treat yourself to something.

Remember, your self-love depends on you. Only you can decide to love yourself or not. Others have no power over your relationship with yourself. Do not hesitate; start practicing your self-love today! It is time to make up your mind to love yourself.

References

Auld, S. (2019, November 4). *Social media and low self-esteem*. ACC Blog. https://www.acc.edu.au/blog/social-media-low-self-esteem/#:~:text=While%20social%20media%20may%20help

Bettino, K. (2021, June 21). *Tips to Soothe Your Worries of What Others Think of You*. Psych Central. https://psychcentral.com/blog/mental-shifts-to-stop-caring-what-people-think-of-you#tips

Bradshaw, M. (2016, September 6). *How to Stop Measuring Your Worth in Achievements*. Tiny Buddha. https://tinybuddha.com/blog/how-stop-measuring-worth-in-achievements/

Capper, J. (2018). *Self-Love and Depression: Loving Yourself Through Recovery*. HealthyPlace. https://www.healthyplace.com/blogs/mentalhealthforthedigitalgeneration/2018/6/self-love-and-depression-loving-yourself-through-recovery

Greenberg, M. (2015). *The 3 Most Common Causes of Insecurity and How to Beat Them*. Psychology Today. https://www.psychologytoday.com/us/blog/the-mindful-self-express/201512/the-3-most-common-causes-insecurity-and-how-beat-them

Guttman, J. (2019, June 27). *The Relationship With Yourself.* Psychology Today. https://www.psychologytoday.com/us/blog/sustainable-life-satisfaction/201906/the-relationship-yourself

Ivanovic, N. (2017, May 15). *Social Media Detox: 13 Ways to Wean Yourself Off Social Media*. LovePanky – Your Guide to Better Love and Relationships. https://www.lovepanky.com/my-life/better-life/social-media-detox

Kolonko, C. (2022, April 14). *How Does Self-Esteem Relate to Depression?* Psych Central. https://psychcentral.com/depression/is-low-self-esteem-making-you-vulnerable-to-depression#next-steps

MindTools. (n.d.). *MindTools Home.* www.mindtools.com. https://www.mindtools.com/air49f4/using-affirmations

R. Morgan Griffin. (2012, August 7). *10 Natural Depression Treatments.* WebMD; WebMD. https://www.webmd.com/depression/features/natural-treatments

RTOR. (2018, April 24). *Why "Love Yourself" Is Good Advice to Follow When Struggling With Mental Health.* Resources to Recover. https://www.rtor.org/2018/04/24/love-yourself/

Says, S. D. (2018, November 5). *The 10 Branches of Self-Love.* The Ladies Coach – Love, Life & Relationship Advice for the Modern Woman. https://theladiescoach.com/spirituality-and-self-love/the-10-branches-of-self-love/

Social. (n.d.). *20 Self Esteem Statistics That Will Help You Feel Better - Soocial.* Social. https://www.soocial.com/self-esteem-statistics/

Steber, C. (2016, May 6). *11 Tips For Letting Go Of A Toxic Friendship, Even If It Seems Impossible.* Bustle; Bustle. https://www.bustle.com/articles/159131-11-tips-for-letting-go-of-a-toxic-friendship-even-if-it-seems-impossible

Taylor, L. (2020, August 10). *51 Self-Love Affirmations to Feel & Attract More Love.* Taylor's Tracks. https://www.taylorstracks.com/self-love-affirmations/

Wanderlust Worker. (2019). *The Importance of Failure: 5 Valuable Lessons from Failing | Wanderlust Worker.* Wanderlustworker.com. https://www.wanderlustworker.com/the-importance-of-failure-5-valuable-lessons-from-failing/

Wisner, W. (2019, June 8). *I Hate Myself: 11 Ways to Combat Self-Loathing.* Talkspace. https://www.talkspace.com/blog/i-hate-myself-stop-self-loathing/